How to Meet the Web Content Accessibility Guidelines

Luke McGrath

ISBN: 978-1-3999-7974-0

Cover Design by Natallie Loseva (bizarreamie.com)

Layout by Stewart Williams

1st Edition 2024

www.wuhcag.com

For Nina, Vani & Anvi.
You made this book possible.

Table of **Contents**

Preface

Updates to the Web Content Accessibility Guidelines are a long time in the making, as was writing this edition of my book.

I've been writing about web accessibility since 2011, when I first needed to research the guidelines for a job I was working at the time. The job came and went, but my fascination with the guidelines and how they can help make the web a better place remained.

With the Web Content Accessibility Guidelines 2.2, the W3C has made a huge leap in simplifying their recommendations and providing working examples of compliance. With each version of their guidelines, they improve not only the web but our chances of meeting their ambitions.

Perhaps at some point there won't be a space for me or my book. Yet, the nature of the guidelines leaves room for interpreters like me to help in what little way I can – to provide my explanations and tips for meeting these standards.

My ambition is that this book contains everything you need and nothing you don't. I try and keep to the simplest and most effective ways to meet the Web Content Accessibility Guidelines.

Thank you for your commitment to making your own projects accessible to all.

Why do we need guidelines?

It's a fair question. Why do we need the Web Content Accessibility Guidelines? Isn't the web an open and equal forum for all?

Yes and no.

In its purest form, HTML code is accessible - web browsers can interpret it and assistive technology (such as screen readers or magnifiers) can adapt it to the needs of a user.

But the web has grown beyond the simple HTML template of old. Websites are now multimedia, real-time and full of invention. The good news is that making a website accessible doesn't mean removing all of this - it just requires a little more thought.

Your users have a range of abilities.

It's not the place of this book to seek to define ability, but for the purposes of understanding it helps to have a working knowledge of the challenges your users may face.

There are broadly four categories to consider:

- Sight - including blind, partially-sighted and colour-blind users.
- Hearing - including deaf and hard of hearing users.
- Motor - including users with reduced, slow or impaired movement.
- Cognitive - including users with impaired concentration, memory or understanding.

This may be a wider definition than you were expecting. In fact, according to the 2021 UK census almost 18% of adults identify as having some form of disability[1].

---

1 www.ons.gov.uk/peoplepopulationandcommunity/healthandsocialcare/healthandwellbeing/bulletins/disabilityenglandandwales/census2021

Personally, I find it difficult to concentrate if there are too many movements and sounds on a webpage, and I struggle to tell the difference between certain colours. Others have much more pronounced challenges, but many more of us than you might think need consideration if you expect us to use your website in the way you want us to.

That's where the guidelines come in. Correctly implemented they're a win-win. Users get a better experience and you get more of whatever it may be your website is intended to do – whether that's selling socks or sharing the latest fishing news.

What is web accessibility?

Web accessibility is simply making your website usable by as many people as possible.

I know what you're thinking, *but that's what I wanted anyway.*

We all do, but there are specific points that you need to understand in order to include everyone you want to. Not only is that valuable market share worth your attention, excluding them could mean breaking equality laws in your country.

This is where the Web Content Accessibility Guidelines come into the picture. They are an internationally recognised and adopted standard for making websites accessible. In many countries, they map neatly to equality and anti-discrimination laws.

Since launching in 1999 the W3C has overseen several iterations of the guidelines. These have evolved as technology has improved and our understanding of web accessibly has increased.

The current guidelines are organised into three levels of conformance:

- Level A - the most basic accessibility features
- Level AA - covers the most common barriers for users
- Level AAA - the highest and most complex solutions

For most cases, Level AA is the standard to aim for as many governments use this as a benchmark. In addition, some websites by the nature of their content cannot reach Level AAA. That said, please don't ignore the highest level when you are ready.

The guidelines are broken up into four principles:

- Perceivable – helps people consume your website
- Operable – helps people use your website
- Understandable – helps people understand your website
- Robust – helps assistive technology interact with your website

The guidelines are spread across these principles, with the majority shared between Perceivable, Operable and Understandable. To reach a Level AA standard of conformance, you'll need to meet guidelines in each of the four principles.

How to use this guide

I have designed this guide to provide you with clear and simple ways to understand and meet each guideline.

Whether you are building a new website or auditing an existing one, this guide will help you review each page and create an action plan to ensure it is accessible.

As I wrote in the preface, this guide doesn't pretend to list every possible way of meeting a guideline. Instead, we'll focus on the most applicable solutions.

I have given each guideline its own chapter with some common sections to make your life easier:

- A statement of the conformance level (A, AA or AAA)
- An explanation of why the guideline exists
- How to pass the guideline
- Exceptions to consider
- Tips for faster and better conformance
- Linked guidelines for easy reference

You should note that following this guide doesn't necessarily mean your website is completely accessible, there are simply too many technologies, permutations and variations to promise you that.

However, this is my interpretation of the best ways to meet the Web Content Accessibility Guidelines. I hope you find it useful.

Let's begin.

Principle 1 - Perceivable

Present all content to users in ways they can perceive.

As you'll learn, users perceive websites in a variety of ways depending on how they choose to browse the internet.

This includes using assistive technology such as screen readers and text-to-speech software, as well as changing contrast, colour or zoom within a browser.

Users must be able to perceive your website in the way that best suits them.

Guideline 1.1 - Text Alternatives

Provide text alternatives for non-text content so that users can adapt the content into the format that best suits their needs.

As with the overall Principle 1, this means providing your content in a way that a user can perceive it through assistive technology or personalised browser settings.

Level A

1.1.1 - Non-text Content

Provide text alternatives for non-text content that serves the same purpose.

Users who cannot see images, hear audio or watch video benefit from having text alternatives in their place. These can be read by the user or voiced by assistive technology.

Text alternatives must provide the same information as the non-text content.

How to Pass

- Add a text alternative to your images describing the image
- For video and audio, at least add a short description of the media but ideally provide a transcript
- Where a control or input field is non-text, add a name

Exceptions

For the following examples, you must provide a text alternative, but it doesn't have to give the same information as the non-text content.

- Tests (if it would invalidate the test)
- CAPTCHA (but provide an accessible alternative, or even better don't use CAPTCHA)

For these final examples, implement them in a way assistive technology can ignore them by using blank alt text.

- Decorative content that has no meaning
- Content used solely for visual formatting
- Content that's invisible to all users

Tips

For images, the alt text should describe the image and give the same information as the image would if seen. This isn't always easy, and people don't always agree on what the 'same' information is. Ask yourself: what does the picture convey?

If the image is your company logo, your company name is a good bet. If the image is of text, replicate the text exactly. For all other images, describe the image helpfully and succinctly: we don't need to know it's a picture of 17,387 trees if the word 'forest' will serve the same purpose.

If you do use CAPTCHA, use one with an audio alternative and add your contact details somewhere close by to help your users if they get stuck.

Blank (or null) alt text is as easy as adding an alt tag with no space between the quotes:

<img src="location-of-image.jpg" alt="" />

Screen readers will skip the image rather than reading the filename or trying to substitute an alt text.

See Also
- 1.4.5 - Images of Text
- 1.4.9 - Images of Text (No Exception)
- 4.1.2 - Name, Role, Value

Guideline 1.2 - Time-based Media

Provide alternatives for video and audio content.

This guideline is all about presenting video and audio content in ways that users can perceive if they prefer to consume them in alternate formats.

It covers assistance like transcripts, captions and audio description for both recorded and live media.

Level A

1.2.1 – Audio-only and Video-only (Pre-recorded)

Provide an alternative to video-only and audio-only content.

Users who have difficulty with hearing and/or vision may need assistance with audio-only or video-only content, such as an audio file, embedded podcast or silent film.

By providing the same information in a different format, these users can access the content by other means, such as text or assistive technology.

How to Pass

- Provide a text transcript that conveys the same information as audio-only media;
- Provide a text transcript that conveys the same information as video-only media; or
- Provide an audio track that conveys the same information as video-only media.

Exceptions

You don't need to provide an alternative if the content *is itself* an alternative for text.

Tips

Sometimes creating a text transcript is simple, other times you have to make a judgement call on what to include. The best bet is, as always, to be honest with your users. What does the media convey and does your transcript do the same? Could you swap one for the other?

A text transcript for a video without sound should describe what is going on in the video as clearly as possible. Try to focus on what the video is trying to say rather than getting bogged down with detail.

Alternatively, for video-only content, record an audio track that narrates the video.

Place your alternative or a link to it directly beneath your video or audio content.

See Also

- 1.2.2 – Captions (Pre-recorded)
- 1.2.3 – Audio Description or Media Alternative (Pre-recorded)
- 1.2.5 – Audio Description (Pre-recorded)
- 1.2.7 – Extended Audio Description
- 1.2.8 – Media Alternative (Pre-recorded)

1.2.2 - Captions (Pre-recorded)

Provide captions for videos with sound.

Users with hearing impairments may not be able to perceive the sound on a video. Presenting the video's information in captions means these users can fully enjoy the content.

How to Pass

- Add captions to all videos with sound.
- Caption all spoken word.
- Identify speakers.
- Caption non-speech information (such as sound effects).

Exceptions

You don't need to provide captions if the video *is itself* an alternative for text. For example, if everything in the video is provided in plain text on the page and the video is the same content but recorded in a video presentation.

Tips

Captions can be closed (hidden until requested) or open (always visible), either will pass this guideline.

There are plenty of paid services that will add captions to your videos, often at reasonable rates. Many free programs will attempt to create your caption file for you, but none as good as human eyes and ears just yet. Like with many areas of web accessibility, your choice is between spending time (writing your own captions) or money (outsourcing).

If you use a lot of videos, build the time into your workflow from the start. If you feel you don't have the time for captions, consider cutting the number of videos you upload. One accessible video that all of your users can enjoy is better than two videos that alienate some of your audience.

See Also

- 1.1.1 - Non-text Content
- 1.2.1 - Audio-only and Video-only (Pre-recorded)
- 1.2.4 - Captions (Live)

Level A

1.2.3 - Audio Description or Media Alternative (Pre-recorded)

Provide audio description or text transcript for videos with sound.

Users who are blind or visually impaired need alternatives for video content.

Adding an audio description track or text transcript helps more users enjoy your content. These both help visually impaired users when the video's regular soundtrack doesn't convey all the information - for example, because the presenter shows items to the camera or demonstrates a process.

How to Pass
- Provide a full-text transcript of the video; or
- Provide a version of the video with an audio description.

Exceptions
- You don't need to satisfy this guideline if the video is itself an alternative to other content.
- You don't need to provide an audio description track if the regular soundtrack contains all the information in the video.

Tips
A text transcript is a document that includes all information present in the video, essentially a script for the video. This means including any visual cues (for example, 'The fisherman holds up a large bass.') as well as dialogue and non-speech sounds.

Audio description is an edited version of a video's soundtrack that adds more information than the regular soundtrack offers during pauses. This might mean narrating movements that are not audibly explained in the video, identifying speakers or explaining visual information. You can provide this to users by letting them select an audio track within the video player or having links to both versions of the video.

Something like a straight face-to-face interview or a speech-to-camera would probably not need audio description. If your video conveys all its information through the regular soundtrack, you don't need to provide an audio description track. Keep this in mind when creating videos.

To meet this guideline, it's easier to provide users with a text transcript instead of an audio description. However, the either/or option only covers Level A. To reach Level AA you need to offer audio description (see 1.2.5) and for Level AAA you need both audio description and text transcript (see 1.2.8).

If you're going to the length of audio description for this guideline, you can also satisfy 1.2.5 - Audio Description (Pre-recorded) and 1.2.7 - Extended Audio Description by recording extended audio description tracks wherever necessary.

See Also
- 1.1.1 - Non-text Content
- 1.2.1 - Audio-only and Video-only (Pre-recorded)
- 1.2.2 - Captions (Pre-recorded)
- 1.2.5 - Audio Description (Pre-recorded)
- 1.2.7 - Extended Audio Description
- 1.2.8 - Media alternative (Pre-recorded)

Level AA

1.2.4 - Captions (Live)
Add captions to live videos.

Users with hearing impairments may rely on captions to enjoy your video content. Adding captions to live videos helps people use your website when you're streaming live video.

How to Pass
Add captions to live video.

Tips
Include presenter cues and important sound effects as well as dialogue. Depending on the software you're using to stream, it may have a built-in auto caption option or you may need to link up some 3rd party captioning software.

This is a difficult and potentially expensive guideline to meet. Broadcasters like the BBC hire professional subtitlers to add captions to live television.

See Also
1.2.2 - Captions (Pre-recorded)

1.2.5 - Audio Description (Pre-recorded)
Provide audio descriptions for pre-recorded videos.

Users with visual impairments or cognitive limitations may rely on audio description to enjoy videos. Adding an audio description soundtrack to videos means these users get all information from the content.

How to Pass
- Provide an audio-described version of a video's soundtrack, selectable by the user; or
- Provide an alternative version of your video with an audio description.

Exceptions
You don't need to add an audio description if your video conveys all its information through the regular soundtrack. Something like a straight face-to-face interview or a speech to-camera would probably not need audio description.

Tips
Audio description is an edited version of a video's soundtrack that adds more information than the regular soundtrack offers during pauses. This might mean narrating movements that are not audibly explained in the video, identifying speakers or explaining visual information. You can provide this to users by letting them select an audio track within the video player or having links to both versions of the video.

Keep this guideline in mind when creating videos to reduce your workload.

If you provided audio descriptions for videos to meet 1.2.3, you've already fulfilled this guideline.

This doesn't apply to live videos or streaming.

See Also
- 1.2.2 - Captions (Pre-recorded)
- 1.2.3 - Audio Description or Media Alternative (Pre-recorded)
- 1.2.7 - Extended Audio Description (Pre-recorded)
- 1.2.8 - Media Alternative (Pre-recorded)

Level AAA

1.2.6 - Sign Language (Pre-recorded)
Provide sign language translations for pre-recorded videos.

Users with hearing impairments can benefit from seeing a sign language translation of your video soundtracks. Users whose first language is a sign language may have limited reading ability, meaning captions can be difficult to follow.

Sign language is also faster to interpret than written captions and can convey emotion and tone much better.

How to Pass
Make an alternative version of your video with a sign language interpreter either present in the main video or embedded as picture-in-picture and link to it from near the original content.

Tips
An obvious issue is which sign language to use. Forms of sign language are often exclusive to a particular country; even British and American sign languages are completely distinct, despite the similarities of the written language.

The best bet is to provide sign language in the language of the country that you are targeting, or if you are multi-national, in the language of the country with the highest proportion of your visitors.

You'll need to find and hire a sign language interpreter for your videos.

See Also
- 1.1.1 - Non-text Content
- 1.2.2 - Captions (Pre-recorded)
- 1.2.3 - Audio Description or Media Alternative (Pre-recorded)

Level AAA

1.2.7 - Extended Audio Description (Pre-recorded)
Provide extended audio descriptions for pre-recorded videos.

Users with visual impairments or cognitive limitations may rely on audio description to enjoy videos. Adding an audio description soundtrack to videos means these users get all information from the content.

For videos where there's more information to convey than the natural pauses in the soundtrack allow you, those users need an extended audio description soundtrack.

How to Pass
- Provide an extended audio-described version of a video's soundtrack, selectable by the user; or
- Provide an alternative version of your video with an extended audio description.

Exceptions
- You don't need to add an audio description at all if your video conveys all its information through the regular soundtrack.
- Something like a straight face-to-face interview or a speech to-camera would probably not need audio description.
- You don't need an extended audio description if regular audio description can provide all of the information in the video during the natural pauses in sound.
- Live videos and streaming.

Tips
Extended audio description builds on audio description by effectively pausing the video to give the soundtrack enough time to pass on all the information from the video. This might mean narrating movements that are not audibly explained in the video, identifying speakers or explaining visual information.

You can provide an extended audio description to users by letting them select an audio track within the video player or having links to both versions of the video.

Keep this guideline in mind when creating videos to reduce your workload.

See Also
- 1.2.3 - Audio Description or Media Alternative (Pre-recorded)
- 1.2.5 - Audio Description (Pre-recorded)
- 1.2.8 - Media Alternative (Pre-recorded)

Level AAA

1.2.8 - Media Alternative (Pre-recorded)
Provide text alternatives for pre-recorded videos.

Users with visual and/or hearing impairments may not be able to perceive the information in a video from its soundtrack or captions.

How to Pass
Provide a full-text transcript for your video and link to it from near the original content

Exceptions
If the video is itself an alternative, you don't need to add a transcript.

Tips
You may have fulfilled this one if you chose to meet 1.2.3 - Audio Description or Media Alternative (Pre-recorded) with a text transcript.

A text transcript is a document that includes all information present in the video, essentially a script for the video. This means including any visual cues (for example, 'The fisherman holds up a large bass.') as well as dialogue and non-speech sounds.

See Also
- 1.2.3 - Audio Description or Media Alternative (Pre-recorded)
- 1.2.5 - Audio Description (Pre-recorded)
- 1.2.7 - Extended Audio Description (Pre-recorded)

Level AA

1.2.9 - Audio Only (Live)
Provide alternatives for live audio.

Some users with hearing impairments may rely on alternatives to enjoy live audio-only content.

How to Pass
- Add captions to live audio; or
- If the live broadcast is from a prepared script, make the script text available from near the original content.

Tips
To add live captions to an audio broadcast, you will need professional software and a trained operator. This isn't a job you can accurately perform without training.

If you can use live video instead, many live streaming platforms now offer auto-captions.

See Also
1.2.4 - Captions (Live)

Guideline 1.3 - Adaptable

Create content that users can consume in different ways.

This guideline is all about giving users control over how your content is presented, so that they can choose the presentation that best suits them.

It covers areas such as the sequencing of content, using sensory characteristics, orientation and identifying the purpose of elements.

Level A

1.3.1 - Info and Relationships

Ensure content and structure is programmatically determinable.

All users benefit when your website structure is logical and each section of content has a clear relationship with the content around it. Visual cues like headings, bullet points, line breaks, tables, bolding, underlining links and other formatting choices help users understand the content.

Assistive technology often relies on correct formatting and logical structures to work. When a user experiences your website through a screen reader, other assistive technology or without CSS they should still understand the content.

How to Pass

Complying with the need for good structure and formatting is a wide-ranging target. Half-measures don't work, so you can't use subheadings properly and then throw random bullet points all over the place.

Amongst other things, you must:

- Break up content with subheadings for new sections
- Mark headings with HTML header tags
- Use lists, tables and other formats where needed
- Use the correct HTML for all structural elements
- Use valid HTML everywhere
- Use clear labels and alternative text on forms

All these elements must be *programmatically determinable* - which means that a web browser or assistive technology can understand them. For example, don't just use bold for headings but use the correct heading tag such as H1.

Where this can't be achieved programmatically, you must provide a text description. For example, "* indicates required fields".

Tips

Ensuring that your web pages have an accessible structure is at once a simple and complex task. The level of difficulty depends on the complexity of your website; a page with several levels of headings will take more work than a single-topic blog post.

An efficient way to check your markup is to use an HTML validator. This will tell you if the web page structure has any HTML errors – these errors won't always equate to accessibility flaws but the cleaner your code the better. Errors like improperly closed paragraph tags are easily remedied.

After using the validator, check pages manually for correctly nested headings and other more visible page elements. Manually check that any forms you use are labelled clearly too, simple things like required field asterisks that lack explanation can cause big problems.

See Also
- 1.3.2 – Meaningful Sequence
- 2.4.3 – Focus Order
- 2.4.6 – Headings and Labels
- 2.4.10 – Section Headings
- 4.1.1 – Parsing

Level AA

1.3.2 - Meaningful Sequence
Present content in a meaningful order.

The meaning of content on your website relies on the order you present it. For example, in English, we read from left to right and read a left-hand column before a right-hand column.

Users who rely on assistive technology (such as a screen reader) to interpret content, require content to be presented in a meaningful order. If this is presented out of sequence, users may become disorientated and may not understand the content.

How to Pass
Ensuring you present your content in a meaningful sequence is a wide-ranging part of web accessibility. It applies to all elements of all pages, so is as big or as small a task as your website.

A sequence is "meaningful" if the order of the content within it cannot be changed without altering its meaning.

Make sure you:

- Present all content in a meaningful order
- Separate navigation menus from the content
- Use paragraphs in order
- Nest headings from H1 downwards to show their relative importance
- Choose whether a list needs numbering or not
- Use valid HTML

Tips
Invest in some assistive technology and use it to browse your website. Turn off the site's Cascading Style Sheet (CSS) and check that your web page displays in the correct order.

Not all content has a meaningful sequence - for example, a sidebar next to the main article where it doesn't matter if the user reads the sidebar or the article first.

Using headings to show importance isn't always straightforward. Headings on a web page are a great way to break up content and show your users the relative importance of each section. Headings in HTML range from H1 (the most important) to H6 (the least important). It's best to have just one Heading1 (H1) on a web page, to show the title of that page.

However, headings don't need to descend from 1 to 6 each time you use one. As well as headings that share levels, you can skip levels altogether if that fits your content.

See Also
- 1.3.1 - Info and Relationships
- 2.4.2 - Page Titled
- 2.4.3 - Focus Order
- 2.4.6 - Headings and Labels

1.3.3 – Sensory Characteristics
Don't use instructions that rely solely on sensory characteristics.

"Sensory characteristics" is an important but complicated-sounding phrase in web accessibility. Thankfully, it's actually far less complicated than it sounds. The sensory characteristics of components are things like shapes, sounds, positioning, orientation, sound, colour and size.

You'll often come across sensory characteristics in instructions to users. Saying things like "Use the search bar on the right" isn't helpful to a user who doesn't understand what 'right' is and "Click the green button" doesn't help users who can't see green.

How to Pass
Getting sensory characteristics right is mainly a case of using your common sense. There are no technical requirements, just good and sensible copywriting:

- Use text labels for elements in addition to sensory characteristics
- Don't use instructions that only use sensory characteristics
- Avoid instructions that rely on sound

Tips
Creating accessible instructions is great for everyone. The clearer your instructions are, the more likely users will follow them.

Good instruction will use several sensory characteristics. Consider the accessibility of these examples:

- 'Use the search box'
- 'Use the search box on the right'
- 'Search by using the green rectangular box labelled 'Search' at the top right of the page'

The first two won't pass, they don't give users enough information. The third uses text labelling to help the user.

We often have an aversion to adding words, feeling that they can confuse users. In this case, the opposite is true. When you need instructions, make them count.

Avoid sound for instructions. It's always hard to tell what the sound
means and what a user did to make it happen. A prime example is if you
use sounds to alert users to errors on a form. The user can't tell exactly
what made the error, they can't even be sure the sound indicated an
error. Use visual cues instead such as colour and symbols.

By making sure you don't rely solely on colour in your instructions, you
can work towards 1.4.1 - Use of Colour.

See Also

1.4.1 - Use of Colour

Level AA

1.3.4 - Orientation
Adapt your website to portrait and landscape views.

Some users have a preferred orientation (portrait or landscape) or physical requirements and need content to adapt to their preference. Others have visual impairments and may find one orientation easier to use.

Most websites pass this guideline as they are responsive and adapt to the user's chosen orientation.

How to Pass
- All content retains meaning when switching orientation
- All content retains function when switching orientation

Exceptions
When a single orientation is essential, for example:

- A landscape image that would be too small to see in portrait mode
- Where the width or height of one orientation is necessary for its function

Level AA

1.3.5 - Identify Input Purpose

Ensure the purpose of input fields are programmatically determinable.

All users, but particularly those with cognitive impairments, benefit from *programmatically determinable* input fields. These allow assistive technologies to understand the purpose of fields and present them in a preferred format to the user.

In addition, users with motor impairments benefit from autocomplete on forms by reducing the need for fine motor movement.

How to Pass
- Specify the intention of each input field with "input type="type"
- Use specific autocomplete values to allow the user's browser to prefill fields where it already has the data

Tips
There's a full list of input purposes that need to be covered at www.w3.org/TR/WCAG22/#input-purposes

Use the most specific label for each field. For example, "bday" rather than "date" if you want a user's date of birth. While the field does want a date, its *purpose* is to collect the birthday.

See Also
1.3.6 - Identify Purpose

Level AAA

1.3.6 - Identify Purpose
Ensure the purpose of components are programmatically determinable.

Users often set personal preferences in their browser or assistive technology to help them understand websites. By ensuring components are understandable by these technologies, users can experience websites in the way that best suits their needs.

Users with cognitive impairments (such as problems with memory, focus, language and decision-making) benefit from this approach. For example, they may set their browser to display a familiar icon for a navigation link or replace your chosen icon for one they understand

How to Pass

- Use ARIA landmarks to define regions of each page
- Use HTML markup to identify links, icons and user interface components

See Also
4.1.2 - Name, Role, Value

Guideline 1.4 - Distinguishable

Make it easy for users to identify and consume content.

This guideline covers 13 ways that you can make your content straightforward for users to find and either read or hear.

It focuses on how users can adapt your content visually to make it easier to consume and separating foreground content from background content.

Level A

1.4.1 - Use of Colour
Don't use presentation that relies solely on colour.

Users with visual impairments, including difficulties perceiving colour, may need help when you use colour on your website to present information.

You can help by using other identifiers such as labels, shapes and patterns.

How to Pass
- Ensure no instructions rely on colour alone
- Ensure that no information (like charts and graphs) relies on colour alone

Tips
Check for colour issues by viewing your website in black and white. Are there any instructions you can't follow or is there information you can't understand?

Making your website accessible to colour-blind users is simple. The main area to focus on is giving instructions. Saying things like 'Click the green button' or 'Required fields are red' is useless to users who can't see green or red. Reinforce these instructions with at least one more identifying remark.

A common failure is link text. Marking this out with a change of colour alone isn't good enough, use an underline, bolding or a symbol too.

Another point is to make sure that important graphics are not dependent on colour alone. For example, your users might not understand a pie chart where only colour separates the segments. In this case, you should add clear labelling and patterns to the segments.

There's an overlap here with 1.3.3 - Sensory Characteristics. Instructions should always be clear and give your users the detail they need.

See Also
1.3.3 - Sensory Characteristics

1.4.2 – Audio Control
Don't play audio automatically.

Automatically playing sounds can distract and disorientate users, especially those with cognitive impairment or relying on a screen reader.

How to Pass
Don't have any audio that plays automatically.

Exceptions
Although you can technically pass this guideline by adding a pause, mute, or stop function to automatic audio, that's a bad idea. You don't want users searching around your website for the audio control.

There's a further exception on audio that plays for less than three seconds. Ignore this too. Three seconds of audio can still distract users, especially those who have problems maintaining focus.

Tips
Don't be afraid to use audio! It can be great on a website, just let users choose when to play it.

See Also
1.4.7 – Low or No Background Audio

Level AA

1.4.3 - Contrast (Minimum)
Set the contrast ratio between text and background to at least 4.5:1.

All users benefit from a good contrast between the text on your website and the background colour.

Some users with visual impairments need a stronger contrast than others to understand your content, so using the right colours is essential.

How to Pass
Make sure the contrast ratio between your text and background is at least 4.5:1.

Do this by:

- Using a light background and dark text; or
- Using a dark background and light text; and
- Using a colour contrast checker to verify your choice.

Exceptions
- Text that is 18 points or larger (or 14 points or larger, if bold) has a lower minimum contrast ratio of 3:1
- Purely decorative text
- Text that is an incidental part of an image (for example, a man who is reading a newspaper or a landscape that happens to include a street sign)
- Brand logos

Tips
In CSS pixel terms, 14 points is 18.5 pixels and 18 points is 24 pixels.

Picking a contrast of at least 7:1 will also fulfil Guideline 1.4.6 - Contrast (Enhanced) at Level AAA.

Remember to ensure that all colours used conform. This includes links that change colour after being used once, and headings in menus and sidebars, as well as the main content.

Make sure that any embedded charts or images of charts have the minimum contrast between elements (for example, bars, axes and labels).

This guideline also applies to images of text (but you shouldn't be using images of text, see 1.4.5 – Images of Text).

See Also
- 1.4.5 – Images of Text
- 1.4.6 – Contrast (Enhanced)
- 1.4.9 – Images of Text (No Exception)
- 1.4.11 – Non-text Contrast

Level AA

1.4.4 - Resize Text

Enable text resizing up to 200% without losing content or function.

Some users with visual impairments need to resize text to understand it fully.

To help these users, your website should allow for up to a 200% resize of text without dropping any content or functions. This should be accomplished in a browser and therefore not require any assistive technology.

How to Pass

Users can resize text content in their web browser up to 200% without loss of meaning or function.

Exceptions
- Images of text (but don't use images of text because they don't resize well)
- Captions

Tips

As all modern browsers allow for resizing text, a website based on good HTML and CSS should comply.

If your website doesn't resize correctly to at least 200% in a browser, add a feature that enables users to resize text (by CSS) based on three or four predetermined options, including 200%.

Check your website by resizing it to 200% in a variety of browsers.

Make sure your resized text doesn't require the user to scroll horizontally and you fulfil part of 1.4.8 - Visual Presentation for Level AAA.

See Also
- 1.4.5 - Images of Text
- 1.4.8 - Visual Presentation
- 1.4.9 - Images of Text (No Exception)
- 1.4.10 - Reflow

1.4.5 - Images of Text
Don't use images of text.

Users with visual or cognitive impairments may rely on changing font size, colour, alignment or spacing to enjoy your content.

Text allows for this kind of personalisation, but images of text almost always don't.

How to Pass
- Don't use an image of text when you can use plain text
- Display quotes as text rather than images
- Use CSS to style headings as text
- Use CSS to style navigation menus as text

Exceptions
- If using an image of text is essential because you can't achieve the effect with text (for example, presenting a particular example of typography)
- If the presentation can't be achieved with the technology used to build the website
- If the text is part of an image that contains other visual content, such as labels on a diagram
- Purely decorative text
- Brand logos

Tips
Images of text are subject to guidelines on colour contrast - see 1.4.3 - Contrast (Minimum) and 1.4.6 - Contrast (Enhanced).

The exception of the website being built in a technology that doesn't allow the text to be presented as text is removed in 1.4.9 - Images of Text (No Exception) at Level AAA.

See Also
- 1.1.1 - Non-text Content
- 1.4.3 - Contrast (Minimum)
- 1.4.6 - Contrast (Enhanced)
- 1.4.9 - Images of Text (No Exception)

Level AAA

1.4.6 – Contrast (Enhanced)
Set the contrast ratio between text and background to at least 7:1.

All users benefit from a good contrast between the text on your website and the background colour.

Some users with visual impairments need a stronger contrast than others to understand your content, so using the right colours is essential.

While the minimum contrast for Level AA was 4.5:1, for Level AAA it's 7:1. This higher standard of contrast helps a wider range of users read your content.

How to Pass
Make sure the contrast ratio between your text and background is at least 7:1.

Do this by:

- Using a light background and dark text; or
- Using a dark background and light text; and
- Using a colour contrast checker to verify your choice.

Exceptions
- Text that is 18 points or larger (or 14 points or larger, if bold) has a lower minimum contrast ratio of 4.5:1
- If the text is purely decorative
- If the text is an incidental part of an image (for example, a man who is reading a newspaper or a landscape that happens to include a street sign)
- Brand logos

Tips
You may have fulfilled this guideline when you completed 1.4.3 – Contrast (Minimum).

In CSS pixel terms, 14 points is 18.5 pixels and 18 points is 24 pixels.

Remember to ensure that all colours used conform. This includes links that change colour after being used once, and headings in menus and sidebars, as well as the main content.

Make sure that any embedded charts or images of charts have the minimum contrast between elements (for example, bars, axes and labels).

This guideline also applies to images of text (but you shouldn't be using images of text, see 1.4.5 – Images of Text).

See Also
- 1.4.3 - Contrast (Minimum)
- 1.4.5 - Images of Text
- 1.4.9 - Images of Text (No Exception)

Level AAA

1.4.7 - Low or No Background Audio
Ensure audio-only content is clear with no or minimal background noise.

Some users have difficulties with their hearing and won't be able to hear your audio content as clearly as others, especially separating speech from background audio.

You can help by ensuring that your audio is clear. If you have pre-recorded audio-only content, keep background noise to a minimum so that the speaking voices can be heard.

How to Pass
- Make sure your pre-recorded audio doesn't contain any background noise; or
- If there has to be some background noise, it's generally 20 decibels lower than the foreground noise. That's about four times quieter.

Exceptions
Background noise is acceptable if:

- The audio isn't mainly speech (for example, in an audio play, an action scene might have a helicopter blown up by a car)
- The audio is part of a CAPTCHA element (CAPTCHA is a test that separates humans from spambots and is often used in forms)
- The audio is "not vocalization intended to be primarily musical expression such as singing or rapping".[2]
- The background sound can be turned off (but it's better just to comply than add complexity)

Tips
Record your audio in a place you know will be quiet (a room with lots of soft furnishings is best if you haven't got a studio).

Only use good quality audio (you should be doing this anyway if you care about your website).

2 www.w3.org/TR/WCAG22/#low-or-no-background-audio

1.4.8 – Visual Presentation
Offer users a range of presentation options for blocks of text.

Users with visual or cognitive impairments may need to customise the presentation of text on your website to understand and enjoy it.

Some users require a certain background and foreground colour to comfortably read text. Others find long lines or justified text difficult to follow and some find it hard to read text where the lines and paragraphs are close together.

As each user has different needs, providing a range of user-selectable options helps the most people.

How to Pass
The following five features are cumulative, as all must be in place to pass:

1. Users can select background and foreground colours; and
2. Text blocks are no wider than 80 characters; and
3. Text is not justified to both sides of the webpage; and
4. Line spacing is at least space-and-a-half within paragraphs and paragraph spacing is at least 1.5 times larger than line spacing
5. Text can be resized in a browser up to 200% without requiring the user to scroll horizontally

Tips
Add all visual presentation options to the header of your website, so they are some of the first things users interact with.

The BBC's accessibility page (www.bbc.co.uk/accessibility) has a good range of colour and spacing options to cover features 1 and 4.

Feature 4, concerning line and paragraph spacing, can be difficult to understand, so here's a more detailed breakdown:

- Text height must be changeable up to 150% of the default
- Spaces between paragraphs must always be 150% of the spaces between lines of text
- A good option is to give users some presets (like the 'AAA' element on the BBC's accessibility page) of:

- » Default text height, line and paragraph spacing
- » 150% default text height, line and paragraph spacing
- » 200% default text height, line and paragraph spacing

You probably fulfilled feature 5 when you completed 1.4.4 – Resize Text.

See Also

1.4.4 – Resize Text

Level AAA

1.4.9 - Images of Text (No Exception)
Don't use images of text.

Users with visual or cognitive impairments may rely on changing font size, colour, alignment or spacing to enjoy your content.

Text allows for this kind of personalisation, but images of text almost always don't.

How to Pass
- Don't use an image of text when you can use plain text
- Display quotes as text rather than images
- Use CSS to style headings as text
- Use CSS to style navigation menus as text

Exceptions
- If using an image of text is essential because you can't achieve the effect with text (for example, presenting a particular example of typography)
- If the text is part of an image that contains other visual content, such as labels on a diagram
- Purely decorative text
- Brand logos

Tips
You may already comply, depending on how you addressed 1.4.5 - Images of Text. The only difference is that 1.4.9 removes the exception that the presentation can't be achieved with the technology used to build the website.

Images of text are subject to colour contrast rules - see 1.4.3 - Contrast(Minimum) and 1.4.6 - Contrast (Enhanced).

See Also
- 1.1.1 - Non-text Content
- 1.4.3 - Contrast (Minimum)
- 1.4.5 - Images of Text
- 1.4.6 - Contrast (Enhanced)

Level AA

1.4.10 - Reflow
Ensure content retains meaning and function without scrolling in two dimensions.

Some users with visual impairments need to resize text to read it comfortably.

When users enlarge content up to 400% of the default size, they should not have to scroll in their browser in more than one direction – horizontally *and* vertically.

How to Pass
- Ensure vertical content doesn't require a horizontal scroll at a width of 320 CSS pixels
- Ensure horizontal content doesn't require a vertical scroll at a height of 256 CSS pixels

Exceptions
- Where multi-directional scrolling is essential for meaning or function (for example images, maps, diagrams, games and components that require toolbars to remain in view)
- Complex data tables

Tips
Responsive web design, where content reflows to fit the user's viewport, may already mean your website complies with this guideline.

It's best not to use horizontal scrolling when writing in most languages, as we are accustomed to reading columns of text vertically. Reflow your content into a single vertical column when enlarged.

320 CSS pixels is the same as a default viewport of 1280 pixels enlarged 400%.

256 CSS pixels is the same as a default viewport of 1024 pixels enlarged 400%.

See Also
1.4.4 - Resize Text

1.4.11 - Non-text Contrast

Set the contrast ratio between user interface components, graphics and adjacent colours to at least 3:1.

All users benefit from a good contrast between the components on your website and the colours around them.

Some users with visual impairments need a stronger contrast than others to fully distinguish and use components such as input fields, buttons and controls, so getting your colour choice right is essential.

How to Pass
- Ensure user controls have a contrast of at least 3:1 to the colour around them;
- Where controls change colour on focus or use, ensure the colours used have a contrast of at least 3:1; and
- Ensure all graphics (for example icons, graphs and charts) have a contrast of at least 3:1 to the colour around them.

Exceptions
- Where a user interface component is visible but inactive (for example, a disabled button)
- A graphic is not required for understanding (for example, a chart where labels give the same information as the coloured lines or a decorative graphic)
- Brand logos
- Representations of other things, such as a screenshot of a website or a heat map

Tips
Remember the different states a component may have and ensure they all comply.

Where form fields use an indicator (for example for missing information), use a colour that meets the contrast criteria.

Where fields or controls use a border, ensure the border meets the criteria.

For graphs, ensure each line or bar has a 3:1 contrast with both the background and the other lines or bars.

For pie charts, ensure each segment has a 3:1 contrast with both the background and the segment on either side of it.

See Also
- 1.4.1 - Use of Colour
- 1.4.3 - Contrast (Minimum)
- 1.4.6 - Contrast (Enhanced)

1.4.12 - Text Spacing

Ensure content and function retain meaning when users change elements of text spacing.

Users with visual or cognitive impairments may wish to amend the default spacing around text content to make it easier for them to read and understand. When they do so, the content should remain visible in full.

How to Pass
Content and function remain intact when a user changes:

- Line height to at least 1.5 times the font size;
- Paragraph spacing to at least 2 times the font size;
- Letter spacing to at least 0.12 times the font size; and
- Word spacing to at least 0.16 times the font size.

Exceptions
- Video captions
- Image of text

Tips
For the most part, a website written in good HTML and CSS will comply. The key here is not having anything that prevents the user from making the changes to spacing.

See Also
1.4.8 - Visual Presentation

1.4.13 - Content on Hover or Focus

Ensure hover or focus triggered content is dismissible, hoverable and persistent.

Additional content triggered by keyboard focus or mouse hover can cause accessibility issues for users with visual or cognitive impairments. Additional content can surprise users, prevent them from completing a task or obscure content.

To overcome these issues, users must be able to understand when additional content appears and dismiss it.

How to Pass

Where keyboard focus or mouse hover triggers additional content to appear, the content must be:

- Dismissible by the user without moving keyboard focus or mouse hover (for example by pressing the 'escape' key or closing on click);
- Hoverable by the mouse pointer so the pointer can be moved over the content; and
- Persistent until the user changes keyboard focus or mouse hover, dismisses the content or the content is no longer valid.

Exceptions

- Where the content communicates an input error
- Where the content doesn't obscure other content
- Where the additional content is controlled by the user. For example, tooltips or sub-menus that appear on mouse hover which are controlled by web browser settings.

Tips

Try not to use this type of content if you can avoid it - add your additional content to the page.

See Also

- 2.1.1 - Keyboard Focus
- 3.2.1 - On Focus

Principle 2 - Operable

Ensure interface components and navigation are operable.

Now that we've covered the ways we can ensure users perceive your website, we move on to the actions they might want to complete.

This includes navigating your website with a keyboard or assistive technology, having enough time to perform actions and being able to use all interface components.

Without meeting these guidelines, your users won't be able to interact with your website in the ways you want them to.

Guideline 2.1 - Keyboard Accessible

Make all functionality available from a keyboard.

This guideline covers four key principles of making your website accessible to users who interact by keyboard.

It includes allowing users to navigate everywhere with a keyboard, ensuring they never get trapped and using keyboard shortcuts.

2.1.1 - Keyboard

Ensure all functionality is accessible by keyboard with no specific timings.

Users with visual or motor impairment may navigate your website using only their keyboard or through assistive technology that relies on a keyboard-like interaction with your website.

How to Pass

- Ensure users can access all elements of your website using only a keyboard
- Ensure there are no specific timings needed for keystrokes, for example holding down 'Enter' for three seconds to submit a form

Exceptions

Functions that require a mouse pointer for input. For example, free drawing tools and some types of games.

Tips

To test for this guideline, unplug your mouse and make sure you can fully use your website with only your keyboard - you might be surprised by what you can't do.

Make sure no function on your website requires timed keystrokes (for example, 'double tap on enter within two seconds').

Don't use 'access keys' (assigning a navigation link to a particular key) or page-specific key commands as they can conflict with assistive technology.

At Level AAA, 2.1.3 - Keyboard (No Exception) removes the exception.

See Also

- 2.1.2 - No Keyboard Trap
- 2.1.3 - Keyboard (No Exception)
- 2.4.3 - Focus Order
- 2.4.7 - Focus Visible

Level A

2.1.2 – No Keyboard Trap

Ensure users can navigate to and from all content using a keyboard.

Users with visual or motor impairments may choose to access your website with only their keyboard. Users must be able to navigate to and away from all content and functionality on your website using a keyboard.

How to Pass

All elements on your website can be navigated to and away from by keyboard only using the 'tab' or arrow keys.

Tips

To test for this guideline, unplug your mouse and make sure you can fully use your website with only your keyboard.

It's tempting to use non-standard navigation with an explanation of what to do, but this isn't worth your time. Stick to the 'tab' and arrow keys that most users are familiar with.

See Also

2.1.1 - Keyboard

2.1.3 - Keyboard (No Exception)
Ensure all functionality is accessible by keyboard with no exceptions.

Users with visual or motor impairment may navigate your website using only their keyboard or through assistive technology that relies on a keyboard-like interaction with your website.

How to Pass
- Ensure users can access all elements of your website using only a keyboard
- Ensure there are no specific timings needed for keystrokes, for example holding down 'Enter' for three seconds to submit a form

Tips
This builds on 2.1.1 - Keyboard by removing the exceptions.

To test for this guideline, unplug your mouse and make sure you can fully use your website with only your keyboard – you might be surprised by what you can't do.

Make sure no function on your website requires timed keystrokes (for example, 'double tap on enter within two seconds').

Don't use 'access keys' (assigning a navigation link to a particular key) or page-specific key commands as they can conflict with assistive technology.

If you have something that, by its nature, must be mouse-controlled (like mouse testing software or a game) then do everything else you can to make your website accessible. Don't panic because you can't comply with this one guideline.

See Also
- 2.1.1 - Keyboard
- 2.1.2 - No Keyboard Trap

2.1.4 - Character Key Shortcuts

Allow users to turn off or remap single-key character shortcuts.

Keyboard shortcuts can help some users, but cause difficulty for those using speech input and some users with motor impairments. They can also cause issues on mobile screens as the functional area is reduced on a mobile keyboard.

For speech input users, single-key character shortcuts (for example, the letter key "F" for starting a search) are particularly bad as a spoken word can be interpreted as several individual keystrokes.

The best course of action is to avoid using single-key character shortcuts.

How to Pass
- Don't use single-key character shortcuts
- If you really want to:
  - » give users a way to turn off the shortcut;
  - » allow users to remap the shortcut to use non-character keys; or
  - » ensure the shortcut only works when an element has focus.

Exceptions
- Shortcuts where one key is not a character (for example 'alt' or 'alt' + 'c')
- Elements where the shortcut is only active on focus (for example, lists and dropdown menus).

Tips
One last time, please just avoid setting up single-key character shortcuts.

Characters include letters, numbers, punctuation and symbols – anything you could type into a word processor and print off.

See Also
3.2.1 – On Focus

Guideline 2.2 - Enough Time

Provide users enough time to read and use content.

This guideline covers six areas that all focus on making sure users have enough time to complete tasks on your website.

It includes allowing users to adjust time limits, removing limits altogether and dealing with re-authentication.

2.2.1 – Timing Adjustable
Provide user controls to turn off, adjust or extend time limits.

Users with visual, motor or cognitive impairments may need more time than others to understand and use your website. Any time controls or limits can make using your website difficult for these users.

How to Pass
If content on your website uses a time limit:

- Give users an option to turn off the time limit before it begins (for example, a landing page before the time-limited page can display a message that shows users what to do); or
- Give users the option to adjust the time limit before it begins, over a range of at least ten times the default setting (you can do this with a landing page too); or
- Give users the option to extend the period at least twenty seconds before it expires. This must be a simple action like clicking a button and must be available to use at least ten times.

If your website has moving or animating text, users must be able to pause the movement.

If your website has a feature that is automatically updated (for example, with the latest football scores), you must allow users to delay the frequency of the updates by at least ten times the default setting.

Exceptions
- The time limit is due to real-time events, like bidding in an auction or a live stream
- The time limit is essential for your business. For example, a ticket sales website that saves a reservation for ten minutes because demand is high and giving users unlimited time would undermine the business process
- The time limit is more than 20 hours.

Tips
Take as much content outside of time limits as possible but consider your users' security. For example, logging out of an account after a period of inactivity is a positive use of a time limit.

Make sure any user controls you provide are keyboard accessible.

The exceptions of the time limit being essential or over 20 hours are both removed at Level AAA in 2.2.3 - No Timing.

If you use a pop-up to give your users the option to extend a time limit, consider 2.2.4 - Interruptions.

See Also
- 2.2.2 - Pause, Stop, Hide
- 2.2.3 - No Timing
- 2.2.4 - Interruptions
- 2.2.5 - Re-authenticating

2.2.2 - Pause, Stop, Hide

Provide user controls to pause, stop and hide moving and auto-updating content.

Moving or auto-updating content on a website can cause difficulties for users with visual or cognitive impairments. These users may not be able to perceive the information before it changes or may be distracted by the movement.

Alongside avoiding moving content, you can help users by providing them with simple controls.

How to Pass
- Ensure moving, blinking or scrolling content has a control to pause, stop or hide it
- Ensure auto-updating content has a control to pause, stop, hide or control the frequency of updates

Exceptions
- The moving, blinking, scrolling or auto-updating content starts only by user request
- The moving, blinking, scrolling or auto-updating content is not presented in parallel with other content (for example, a full-page advert displayed before users reach your webpage)
- The moving, blinking or scrolling content lasts less than five seconds
- The movement is essential (for example, an animation that shows users that something is loading, if it would otherwise look like your website was frozen)

Tips
When a user pauses and unpauses content, let them continue where they left off if the content is pre-set but take them to the current display if the content is real-time.

A rough guide is that "blinking" content pulses less than three times per second. Anything that pulses faster is "flashing" content and has its own rules (see 2.3.1 - Three Flashes or Below and 2.3.2 - Three Flashes). The distinction falls on the line between what may cause a seizure in a user (flashing) and what is more of a distraction than a hazard (blinking).

My advice is to remove anything that blinks or flashes and never auto-play content - that way you pass without having to build all the controls or time it to five seconds.

See Also
- 2.2.1 - Timing Adjustable
- 2.3.1 - Three Flashes or Below
- 2.3.2 - Three Flashes

2.2.3 – No Timing
Set no time limits.

Users with visual, motor or cognitive impairments may need more time than others to understand and use your website. Any time controls or limits can make using your website difficult for these users.

How to Pass
Ensure there's no time-limited content on your website.

Exceptions
The time limit is due to real-time events, like bidding in an auction or a live stream.

See Also
- 2.2.1 – Timing Adjustable
- 2.2.5 – Re-authenticating

Level AAA

2.2.4 - Interruptions
Enable users to postpone or suppress non-emergency interruptions.

Users with cognitive impairments may have difficulty maintaining their focus and attention. Interrupting their experience can impact their understanding of your content. Those with visual impairments who use a screen reader may struggle if content changes while they are consuming it.

Ideally, avoid these issues by eliminating all non-emergency interruptions.

How to Pass
- Don't interrupt users, other than for emergencies
- If you really want to interrupt users:
  » provide an option for turning off all but emergency interruptions (for example, by a 'preferences' or 'accessibility' page where choices persist for the user's session);
  » allow users to postpone all updates and interruptions; or
  » allow users to request updates rather than receive them automatically.
- Don't use an automatic redirect or refresh function based on a time delay (for example, if a webpage has moved, do not redirect users to the new page after a certain amount of time).

Exceptions
Emergencies include civil emergency alert messages and messages that warn of danger to health, safety, or property – including data loss or loss of connection.

Tips
The best thing you can do is eliminate all interruptions.

If you must use a pop-up, make sure the keyboard focus is on the window-closing 'X' icon in the corner that closes the pop-up. When a user closes a pop-up, return keyboard focus to the place on the page they were at before the pop-up appeared.

There is an overlap with 2.2.1 - Timing Adjustable, which allows for a warning to interrupt a user to tell them that a time limit is approaching as that would count as a loss of connection.

See Also
2.2.1 - Timing Adjustable

2.2.5 - Re-authenticating
Save user data when re-authenticating.

It may be essential for users to re-authenticate their identity for certain functions. For example, you might set a login to expire after a certain amount of time in case a user leaves their computer unattended.

Some users need longer than others to complete tasks on a website. You can help these users by saving the information they enter and when they re-authenticate (such as logging back in), displaying the same data.

How to Pass
When you ask a user to re-authenticate their identity, ensure the user can continue exactly as before with saved data (for example, their shopping basket contents, input into forms or accessibility options).

Tips
Ensure surveys and questionnaires can be saved part-completed and finished later.

If you ask your users to re-authenticate after a certain amount of time, consider whether your use of a time limit is justified under 2.2.1 - Timing Adjustable and 2.2.3 - No Timing. If the limit is for security reasons, such as protecting user data, this will pass both guidelines.

See Also
- 2.2.1 - Timing Adjustable
- 2.2.3 - No Timing

2.2.6 - Timeouts

Warn users about timeouts that cause data loss.

Time limits can cause problems for some users with cognitive impairments, who may take longer to complete tasks on a website. It's therefore important to allow users to complete a process in more than one sitting and alert users to the length of any timeout period.

How to Pass

- Where possible, allow users 20 hours before a timeout removes their data
- Warn users of the duration of any timeout period at the beginning of the task

Tips

There are two main types of timeout, for inactivity or a hard time limit. Inactivity is easier for users to deal with as they may be making progress (albeit at a slower pace) and so will be less likely to trigger the timeout.

Hard time limits can be justified if they protect user data or are essential for a business (for example an auction site or hotel room booking form).

Watch out for privacy regulations when you store data, many countries require explicit positive consent for you to do so.

This guideline overlaps with 2.2.1 - Timing Adjustable, which also deals with time limits and the controls around them.

See Also

2.2.1 - Timing Adjustable

Guideline 2.3 - Seizures and Physical Reactions

Don't publish content in a way known to cause seizures or physical reactions.

This guideline is all about looking after the health of your users and avoiding creating in ways that might harm them.

It covers visual cues that can lead to problems for some people, including flashing and animated content.

2.3.1 - Three Flashes or Below Threshold
Don't flash content more than three times per second.

Flashing content on a website can cause difficulties for users with photosensitive seizure disorders such as epilepsy. Flashing content can cause these users to suffer a seizure.

How to Pass
Don't add anything to your website that flashes more than three times per second.

Exceptions
There's one exception to this guideline based on the size of the flashing content, but I recommend you ignore it and just don't let anything flash more than three times per second.

Here's that exception in full if you're interested:

"the combined area of flashes occurring concurrently occupies no more than a total of .006 steradians within any 10 degree visual field on the screen (25% of any 10 degree visual field on the screen) at typical viewing distance."[3]

If you can understand that you're smarter than me!

Tips
Remember, flashing is different to blinking (see 2.2.2 - Pause, Stop, Hide). Blinking can distract users but doesn't cause seizures.
If blinking content occurs three times per second, it is considered flashing content.

The exception is removed at Level AAA in 2.3.2 - Three Flashes.

See Also
- 2.2.2 - Pause, Stop, Hide
- 2.3.2 - Three Flashes

---

3 www.w3.org/WAI/WCAG21/Understanding/three-flashes-or-below-threshold.html#dfn-general-flash-and-red-flash-thresholds

HOW TO MEET THE WCAG

Level AAA

2.3.2 - Three Flashes
Don't flash content more than three times per second.

Flashing content on a website can cause difficulties for users with photosensitive seizure disorders such as epilepsy. Flashing content can cause these users to suffer a seizure.

How to Pass
Don't add anything to your website that flashes more than three times per second.

Tips
Remember, flashing is different to blinking (see 2.2.2 - Pause, Stop, Hide). Blinking can distract users but doesn't cause seizures.

If blinking content occurs three times per second, it is considered flashing content.

This removes the exception from Level A in 2.3.1 - Three Flashes or Below Threshold.

See Also
- 2.2.2 - Pause, Stop, Hide
- 2.3.1 - Three Flashes or Below Threshold

2.3.3 - Animation From Interactions
Provide users with controls to disable motion animation.

Animations on a website can distract users and, in some cases, cause nausea. Avoiding animated elements triggered by the user (for example parallax scrolling or a 'page loading' animation) can help these users enjoy the website.

How to Pass
- Don't use motion animation on your website; or
- Allow users to disable all non-essential motion animation.

Exceptions
Animation that's essential to a website's function or information, if the same cannot be achieved by other means.

Tips
"Motion animation" means adding steps to states, such as making a bar chart appear to grow from 0 to 100, rather than loading it at 100.

Add a site-wide control to the top of your website to allow the user to turn off non-essential animation.

This doesn't mean websites with animation can't pass, as an animated video would be fine if the purpose of the page was to display that animated video. It's decorative animation you should seek to avoid or allow users to turn off.

See Also
2.2.2 - Pause, Stop, Hide

Guideline 2.4 - Navigable

Provide users with ways to navigate, find content and understand where they are.

This guideline contains 13 different points, all relating to the way users move around your website.

This includes navigation menus, headings, links, focus and much more.

2.4.1 - Bypass Blocks
Provide a way for users to skip repeated blocks of content.

Websites often have the same, or very similar, content at the top of each page (for example the navigation menu, header and certain graphics). Some users with visual, motor or cognitive impairments who navigate sequentially through elements can struggle to get past this repetitive content.

For example:

- screen readers often announce all of the elements on the page to the user in order;
- users who navigate by keyboard might have to key past each link in a menu; and
- users who browse with a lot of zoom can get lost on a page.

To help these users navigate your website, provide a way for them to bypass the repetitive parts of each page.

How to Pass
- Add a visible 'Skip to Content' link to all pages on your website that sends users to the start of the main content on each page; or
- Add a link at the start of any repeated content to skip it; or
- Add links at the start of a page to each area of content.

Tips
While a 'Skip to Content' link will pass this guideline, there is a little more you can do. A standard in HTML5 allows you to label your navigation menu as a <nav> element. Some screen readers can use the <nav> element and provide a way for users to skip menus.

See Also
- 1.3.2 - Meaningful Sequence
- 2.4.2 - Page Titled
- 3.2.3 - Consistent Navigation

Level A

2.4.2 - Page Titled
Use helpful and clear page titles.

All users benefit from descriptive page titles. A good title tells your users which page they are on and what that page is for. This lets users quickly understand if they are on the right page.

Users with visual, cognitive and mobility impairments further benefit as the technology they use can more heavily rely on page titles.

How to Pass
Give each page on your website a unique and descriptive meta title.

Tips
A useful format for writing page titles is 'Page name - Page description - Website name' ('About Us - Learn our Secrets - ACME Corp').

If pages are part of a process, such as a checkout, use the title to tell the user what stage they're at ('Checkout - Page 1 of 5 - ACME Corp').

Don't forget dynamic pages such as search results ('Search Results for XXXX') and 404 errors (Sorry, we can't find that page).

In many cases, it makes sense to repeat the page title or a variation of it as the top heading on your page.

Type your page titles into a spreadsheet and review them. If they make sense out of context, they will work on your website.

Use these page titles in your sitemap (see 2.4.5 - Multiple Ways and 2.4.8 - Location) to make it more accessible.

See Also
- 1.3.1 - Info and Relationships
- 1.3.2 - Meaningful Sequence
- 2.4.5 - Multiple Ways
- 2.4.8 - Location

2.4.3 - Focus Order
Ensure components receive focus in a logical sequence.

Your users need to find their way around your website in a sequential and meaningful order. You can control this with the 'focus order' of your website.

'Focus order' is the sequence in which users access components on your website. Users with keyboard-only navigation or screen readers will follow the focus order you have set, so your focus order must preserve meaning and usability.

How to Pass
Ensure the focus order of each web page follows a sequence that preserves the meaning and functionality of the page.

Exceptions
- Complex items like tree diagrams do not have to be exactly programmed to a specific order if your users can reach every element.
- You don't need to set a focus order if your page doesn't need to be navigated in a particular sequence to be understood. For example, a random collage of links or images.

Tips
Unplug your mouse and verify that you can use the 'Tab' key to navigate to every part of your website and use every function, including search boxes and forms - make sure each page has a sensible focus order.

If you have complied with 2.1.1 - Keyboard, you may have already covered elements of this guideline.

See Also
- 1.3.2 - Meaningful Sequence
- 2.1.1 - Keyboard
- 2.4.7 - Focus Visible

Level A

2.4.4 - Link Purpose (In Context)
Make every link's purpose clear from its text or context.

You must make your links clear and easy to understand, ideally from just the link text itself.

That's because users with assistive technology, like a screen reader, often listen to all the links on a page to help them find where they want to go. Others may view your website highly magnified or tab through links, so they will only see the link text and a few words around it at any one time.

To help your users, your link text (the words that are linked, often called 'anchor text') must make the link destination clear, in the context of their surrounding content.

How to Pass
Make sure that for each link on your website:

- The purpose of the link is clear from the link text (for example, '<u>My blog</u>'); or
- The purpose of the link is clear from the surrounding content, meaning the same sentence, paragraph or cell in a table (for example, 'Visit my <u>blog</u>'); or
- If the link is an image, the alt text of the image makes the link's purpose clear (for example, 'Luke McGrath - Visit my blog'); and
- Links with the same destination have the same description (but links don't share a description if they point to different places).

Exceptions
You don't need to make the link purpose clear if the purpose is ambiguous to *all* your users.

For example, if I link the word 'blog' in the phrase 'I have a personal blog' the link might go to my blog, or it might go to a Wikipedia page explaining what a blog is. No user would reliably know where the link goes before they follow the link.

Of course, it's best to avoid ambiguous links as users should always know where they are going. Although, there are times when you might want to spring a fun surprise on everyone.

Tips

A good writer will only ever need the first option, making the link purpose clear for the link text. It is the most accessible solution and the best for your users. There is always a way to make your link accessible using link text alone.

At Level AAA, 1.4.9 - Link Purpose (Link Only) requires you to make links accessible using only the link text.

Where you link to another page on your website, it's good practice to use the page title you set in 2.4.2 - Page Titled as the link text.

See Also
- 1.1.1 - Non-text Content
- 2.4.2 - Page Titled
- 2.4.9 - Link Purpose (Link Only)

2.4.5 - Multiple Ways
Offer at least two ways to find pages on your website.

All users benefit from a website that makes it easy to find and navigate web pages. Some users will find certain methods easier than others, so it's important to offer a range of options.

For example, users with visual impairments may prefer a search function, whereas those with cognitive impairments may find a sitemap easier to use.

How to Pass
Provide multiple ways for users to find your website's pages by:

- Adding a sitemap page that links to every page on your website; and
- Including a search function on every page (by adding it to the header); and
- Providing a clear and consistent main navigation menu.

Exceptions
- You don't need to provide multiple ways to access pages that users only reach after a certain process (for example, a receipt or confirmation page).
- If your website only has a handful of pages, one clear navigation menu may suffice.

Tips
Though you only need at least two methods available, the three suggested above make a more comprehensive solution.

A good HTML sitemap will depend on the structure of your website. Design your sitemap so that it best reflects the structure of your website pages and contains all your pages.

A 'related pages' section (which shows links to similar pages on your website) is a good way of helping users navigate around your website.

See Also

- 1.4.2 - Page Titled
- 2.4.1 - Bypass Blocks
- 2.4.8 - Location

2.4.6 - Headings and Labels

Ensure headings and labels describe topic or purpose.

A webpage can be broken up with headings or labels where content changes topic, introduces a sub-topic or changes purpose. Where headings or labels are used, they must be descriptive.

Users with low reading ability or short-term memory issues benefit from headings for sections of content to make it clear what the section contains. People who use screen readers may also use headings to navigate to sections.

As well as headings, descriptive labels on form controls help users know how to complete the form fields.

How to Pass
- Use descriptive headings and subheadings in content where appropriate (a change in topic or purpose)
- Use descriptive labels on controls and input fields

Tips
A single letter of the alphabet can be a good heading (for example, in an alphabetical index).

If you regularly produce similar content, keep headings consistent (for example, a website about film reviews might have 'Plot', 'Characters' and 'Verdict' on each page).

Make sure headings can be programmatically determined as required by 1.3.1 - Info and Relationships.

See Also
- 1.3.1 - Info and Relationships
- 1.3.2 - Meaningful Sequence
- 3.3.2 - Labels or Instructions

2.4.7 - Focus Visible
Make keyboard focus visible when active.

Where there are multiple elements on a webpage, it helps users to highlight which element has keyboard focus. This helps users who rely on a keyboard to navigate as it shows them which element the keyboard will interact with. Users with attention or short-term memory limitations will also benefit from a visual cue to where focus is located.

How to Pass
When an element has keyboard focus, show a visual indication.

Tips
For form fields, you might display a bar within the field or highlight the entire field.

For controls, you might display a border around the control.

See Also
- 2.1.1 - Keyboard
- 2.4.3 - Focus Order
- 2.4.11 - Focus Appearance (Minimum)
- 2.4.12 - Focus Appearance (Enhanced)

Level AAA

2.4.8 - Location
Let users know where they are on your website.

Some of your users will have problems understanding the structure of your website. They can get lost, especially during interactions like checkouts that take place over a few pages.

You can help your users by making it clear where they are on your website.

How to Pass
- Use breadcrumbs to help with navigation. Show the sequence a user is following and where they are in that sequence. For example, You are here: Home > Fish > Bass; and
- Add a sitemap page to your website (see 2.4.5 - Multiple Ways) so your users have another way of finding what they want. Add a link to the sitemap somewhere prominent like the header.

Tips
Use full page titles for breadcrumbs when they are 1-3 words long. Abbreviate longer titles to make them easier to read (for example, 'A Guide to Exotic Fish' could just as well be 'Exotic Fish' for a breadcrumb).

For a process that takes a few pages (like a shopping cart), show all the steps in the process and highlight where the user is.

If a page has too many breadcrumbs, perhaps your website could be better organised.

Use your page titles in your sitemap, organised under subheadings.

See Also
- 2.4.2 - Page Titled
- 2.4.5 - Multiple Ways

Level AAA

2.4.9 - Link Purpose (Link Only)
Make every link's purpose clear from its text.

You must make your links clear and easy to understand.

That's because users with assistive technology, like a screen reader, often listen to all the links on a page to help them find where they want to go. Others may view your website highly magnified or tab through links, so they will only see the link text and a few words around it at any one time.

To help your users, your link text (the words that are linked, often called 'anchor text') must make the link destination clear.

How to Pass
Make sure that for each link on your website:

- The purpose of the link is clear from the link text (for example, 'My blog'); or
- If the link is an image, the alt text of the image makes the link's purpose clear (for example, 'Luke McGrath - Visit my blog'); and
- Links with the same destination have the same description (but links don't share a description if they point to different places).

Exceptions
You don't need to make the link purpose clear if the purpose is ambiguous to *all* your users.

For example, if I link the word 'blog' in the phrase 'I have a personal blog' the link might go to my blog, or it might go to a Wikipedia page explaining what a blog is. No user would reliably know where the link goes before they follow the link.

Of course, it's best to avoid ambiguous links as users should always know where they are going. Although, there are times when you might want to spring a fun surprise on everyone.

Tips
You may have passed this if you didn't rely on link context for 2.4.4 - Link Purpose (In Context).
Where you link to another page on your website, it's good practice to use the page title you set in 2.4.2 - Page Titled as the link text.

See Also

- 1.1.1 - Non-text Content
- 2.4.2 - Page Titled
- 2.4.4 - Link Purpose (In Context)

2.4.10 - Section Headings
Organise content with headings.

Adding section headings to all content will help your users understand your website. They are most helpful for users who have difficulty focusing or remembering where they are on a page, as well as users with a visual impairment who may navigate by skipping between headings.

You can help these users, and everyone else, by ensuring that all content on your website is broken up by clear and informative headings.

How to Pass
Add a heading for every new thought or topic in your content (for example, a travel article may have headings to indicate the distinct sections on dining, transportation, and lodging).

Exceptions
A webpage can be a single block of content with only one header if it is about one thought or topic.

Tips
A section is a self-contained portion of written content that deals with one or more related topics or thoughts.

A section may consist of one or more paragraphs and include graphics, tables, lists and sub-sections.

Beware of making your content harder to read by forcing in too many headings.

Certain content may not be able to meet this guideline. For example, if your website publishes unabridged historical documents that don't use headings.

See Also
- 1.3.1 - Info and Relationships
- 1.3.2 - Meaningful Sequence
- 2.4.6 - Headings and Labels

2.4.11 – Focus Not Obscured (Minimum)
Keep elements visible when focused on.

It seems simple and sensible, but it is crucial to ensure elements that receive focus are visible to users.

Users with mobility impairments, particularly those who do not use a mouse, need to see which element has focus. If this is not visible to them, they may not know how to proceed..

How to Pass
When an element receives focus, it is at least partially visible.

Tips
If an element is movable by a user, only the starting position of that element is required to be visible.

If content is opened by the user which then obscures elements, this is not a fail as long as the content can be dismissed or closed.

While this guideline requires only partial visibility, you can meet 2.4.12 - Focus Not Obscured (Enhanced) at Level AAA by ensuring elements are fully visible.

Watch out for pop ups, modals and sticky navigation which can overlap and obscure elements.

See Also
- 1.4.11 - Non-text Contrast
- 2.4.7 - Focus Visible
- 2.4.12 - Focus Not Obscured (Enhanced)

2.4.12 - Focus Not Obscured (Enhanced)
Keep elements fully visible when focused on.

It is important to ensure elements that receive focus are fully visible to users.

Users with mobility impairments, particularly those who do not use a mouse, need to see which element has focus. If this is not fully visible to them, they may not know how to proceed.

How to Pass
When an element receives focus, it is fully visible.

Tips
Think about the viewport area of your website if using sticky navigation and ensure it doesn't overlap.

For pop ups, such as cookie consent, ensure they are modal, receive focus and can be dismissed.

See Also
- 1.4.11 - Non-text Contrast
- 2.4.7 - Focus Visible
- 2.4.11 - Focus Not Obscured (Minimum)

Level AAA

2.4.13 - Focus Appearance
Make sure focus indicators are easy to recognise.

It is important to make it clear to users when an element receives focus. Knowing where focus is enables users to interact with or navigate past an element.

Users with impairments in their sight may need help to recognise where focus is. Making the indicator large and with good contrast can help these users.

How to Pass
Ensure that keyboard focus indicators have:

- a border that is at least 2 CSS pixels large

- at least 3:1 contrast ratio with the unfocused state

Exceptions
- Where the focus indicator is determined by web browser or other user agent

- Where the focus indicator and the background colour are not set by the website creator

Tips
- The most common form of indicator is a border surrounding an element.

- A 3:1 contrast ratio is the minimum requirement, but consider increasing this to better help users.

- Remember that text links are elements, not just buttons and controls.

See Also
- 1.4.11 - Non-text Contrast
- 2.4.7 - Focus Visible

Guideline 2.5 - Input Modalities

Make it easy for people to use your website beyond a keyboard.

This guideline contains eight sections, all relating to different ways a user might interact with your website.

This includes many actions related to mouse pointers.

Level A

2.5.1 - Pointer Gestures

Enable multi-point and path-based gestures to be operated with a single pointer.

Some users cannot easily perform gestures in a reliable or precise way, which can make it difficult for them to interact with websites where gestures are required. To overcome this, users might have assistive technology driven by speech or eye movement to make gestures.

Multi-point or path-based movements can be particularly challenging for some users. A multi-point gesture is one where two or more gestures are needed together. For example, a two-finger pinch and zoom or swipe. A path-based movement might be drawing a shape or swiping through a carousel.

How to Pass

Where you have a function that requires a multi-point or path-based gesture, provide a way for a user to operate the same function with a single pointer.

For example:

- Where a map might use pinch and zoom it can also have + and – controls operated by a single click or tap.
- A carousel operated by a series of swipes can also have 'forward' and 'back' buttons

Exceptions

Where a multi-point or path-based gesture is essential for functionality. For example, drawing a signature on a document.

Tips

This goes beyond providing a keyboard-accessible control as some users find pointers easier to use than keyboards. A user with an eye movement pointer will often find it easier to point at a control than to switch to a keyboard.

See Also

2.5.7 - Dragging

LUKE McGRATH

Level A

2.5.2 - Pointer Cancellation
Ensure functions don't complete on the down-click of a pointer.

Some users may need extra help using a mouse or prefer to use assistive technology in place of a mouse. It's important to reduce the chances of an accidental click for these users by ensuring that the down-click of a mouse pointer alone doesn't complete a function.

How to Pass
- Ensure that actions are only taken when a pointer is clicked and released within the boundary of the target.
- Abort actions where the pointer is released outside the boundary of the target.

Exceptions
Where the action must occur on the down-click.

This might seem rare but is relevant to keyboard emulators, where a letter appears typed on the down-press of a key (and therefore the down-press of a mouse in an emulator). A music keyboard or shooting game may also need the action to complete on the down-click.

2.5.3 – Label in Name

Ensure that text labels for components match the name of the component.

Some users rely on the programmatic names of components and controls, rather than text that is visually displayed on them. This is especially useful for users relying on assistive technology such as screen readers as the name of the control and the text displayed on it will match.

For speech-input users, mismatched labels and names may prevent them from effectively interacting with a control as they will need to use a name different to that displayed.

How to Pass

- Ensure that the text label and programmatic name of components match.
- Abort actions where the pointer is released outside the boundary of the target.

Exceptions

- Where there is no visible label for a component.
- Where text is used symbolically, for example if 'ABC" is used to indicate a spellchecker.

Tips

Labels include:
- Text to the left of dropdown lists and text inputs
- Text to the right of checkboxes and radio buttons
- Text inside buttons and tabs
- Text below icons used as buttons

Programmatic names include alt text, aria-label and aria-labelledby attributes.

Programmatic names can be simplified versions of the display text if they begin with the same word. For example, 'Search this page' could use a name 'Search'.

When deciding how much text counts as a visual label, take a commonsense approach. The text immediately adjacent to the control will be enough.

2.5.4 - Motion Actuation

Ensure functions operated by motion can also be operated through an interface and responding to motion can be disabled.

Where gestures such as pointing or movements like shaking or tilting control a function, some users will need to be able to control these through a more standard interface. Users with mobility impairments may not be able to make the correct movements (or make them precisely enough) to interact with these types of controls.

Similarly, some users may inadvertently use these controls and therefore need a way to switch them off.

How to Pass

- Ensure users can enable and disable gesture and movement-based controls.
- Provide a standard interface (such as a button) in addition to motion and gesture controls.

Exceptions

- Where the motion operates a function through an accessible interface supported by the user's assistive technology and:
- The technology is supported widely (such as HTML); or
- The technology is supported in a widely distributed plug-in; or
- The content is within a closed environment or network where the user agent required is accessible; or
- The user agents that support the technology are available at the same cost and as easily to users with and without disabilities.
- Where the motion is essential for the function, for example, a step counter that uses movement to calculate distance.

Tips

Ignore the exceptions and stick to providing an alternate interface and the ability to disable motion controls.

Level AAA

2.5.5 - Target Size
Ensure the target size for pointer inputs is at least 44 by 44 CSS pixels.

Users with mobility impairments may have difficulty using elements if their target area is small. These users may have trouble with aiming or being able to keep a pointer steady. Larger target areas help these users interact with controls and elements.

How to Pass
Ensure that the target areas for all pointer inputs are at least 44 by 44 CSS pixels.

Exceptions
- When the target is available through an equivalent control on the same page that meets the requirements.
- When the target is a sentence or block of inline text.
- When the target size is controlled by the user agent.
- When the presentation of a target that doesn't meet the requirements is essential.

Tips
Remember that pointers include both mouse control and touch control.

Although there is a minimum size, the larger the control the easier it is for everyone to use.

Consider making frequently used or important controls larger.

Be careful not to place controls near the edge of a screen as this may be more difficult to reach for some users.

Meeting these requirements also meets 2.5.8 - Target Size (Minimum).

See Also
- 2.5.8 - Target Size (Minimum)

2.5.6 – Concurrent Input Mechanisms
Don't restrict modes of input.

Users may choose to switch between different methods of input when interacting with a website. For example, for some controls, a user might prefer to input by keyboard and for others, they might favour a mouse.

Users might also prefer to override the primary input mechanism for a device. For example, connecting an external keyboard to a touchscreen tablet.

How to Pass
Ensure there are no restrictions on modes of input.

Exceptions
- Where a set input mode is essential. For example, a touch-typing test.
- If the restriction is required for security.
- If the restriction is required to respect a user's settings.

Level AA

2.5.7 - Dragging Movements
Ensure functionality that uses dragging can be achieved with a single pointer without dragging.

Some users with mobility impairments may have difficulty using a dragging action precisely, either by mouse pointer or touch. Others may use an accessible input mechanism, such as eye control, that makes dragging even more difficult or even impossible.

These users need an alternative that enables them to complete the same input as dragging.

How to Pass
Where a control uses dragging, provide an alternative.

Exceptions
Where dragging is essential. For example, creating art or playing a game where dragging is a design feature.

Tips
A dragging action is one where only the start and end points matter, the direction between them is not considered.

A common example of a dragging control is one where the user drags elements into a certain order. This can also be achieved by a clickable up/down navigation or by typing numbered values next to elements.

See Also
- 2.1.1 - Keyboard
- 2.1.3 - Keyboard (No Exception)
- 2.5.1 - Pointer Gestures

2.5.8 - Target Size (Minimum)
Ensure the target size for pointer inputs is at least 24 by 24 CSS pixels.

Users with mobility impairments may have difficulty using elements if their target area is small. These users may have trouble with aiming or being able to keep a pointer steady. Larger target areas help these users interact with controls and elements.

How to Pass
Ensure that the target areas for all pointer inputs are at least 24 by 24 CSS pixels.

Exceptions
- When there is at least 24 CSS pixels distance to any adjacent target.
- When the target is a sentence or block of inline text.
- When the target size is controlled by the user agent.
- When the presentation of a target that doesn't meet the requirements is essential.

Tips
Making the spacing of targets at least 44 by 44 CSS pixels will pass 2.5.5 - Target Size at Level AAA.

Remember that pointers include both mouse control and touch control.

Although there is a minimum size, the larger the control the easier it is for everyone to use.

Consider making frequently used or important controls larger.

Be careful not to place controls near the edge of a screen as this may be more difficult to reach for some users.

See Also
- 2.5.5 - Target Size

Principle 3 - Understandable

Make information and controls understandable.

Having mastered making your website perceivable and operable, we now need to ensure users can understand both your content and how to use your website.

This includes ensuring your website is readable, predictable and helps users when they make mistakes.

Without meeting these guidelines, your users won't be able to understand your website.

Guideline 3.1 - Readable

Make text readable and understandable.

This guideline contains six sections, relating to how users will read and understand the text content on your website.

This includes language, unusual words, abbreviations, reading level and pronunciation.

Level A

3.1.1 - Language of Page
Set a default language for each webpage.

For users who rely on conventional web browsers and those who prefer assistive technologies, assigning a webpage's language is essential for understanding.

Among the benefits, the text is rendered more accurately, screen readers will use the correct pronunciation rules and captions will load correctly.

How to Pass
Set the default language of each webpage using the "lang" HTML attribute.

Tips
Set the language in your site template so you only have to do this once (unless your website has pages in different languages).

If a webpage has content in more than one language, set the page to the language used most.

If a webpage uses multiple languages equally, set the page to the language used first.

When using English, be aware of the three options "en", "en-gb" and "en-us". If in doubt, stick with "en" as this lets users set their preference.

See Also
3.1.2 - Language of Parts

3.1.2 - Language of Parts
Set a default language for each part of a webpage.

If your website has content in a different language to its main language, you should tell your users about the change. This helps browsers render the content correctly and assistive technology, such as screen readers, to interpret content accurately.

How to Pass
- Set the default language of each webpage using the "lang" HTML attribute; and
- Add a further "lang" attribute to content that is not in the main language.

Exceptions
- Words that have become part of the main language (for example, 'rendezvous' is used in English but is of French origin).
- Proper names.
- Technical terms.
- Words of indeterminate language.

Tips
If you have an alternative language version or translation of some content, link to it with the name of the language in that language (for example, 'Francais', 'Deutsch') and add a language tag to the link.

See Also
3.1.1 - Language of Page

Level AAA

3.1.3 - Unusual Words
Define any unusual words or phrases.

Some of your users will find it hard to read unusual uses of words on your website. Things like figurative language, idioms and jargon can be difficult to process. Users who read your content zoomed-in may struggle with unusual words if they can't see the context around them.

Avoid using unusual words where you can and explain the use of words when you need to use them.

How to Pass
- Avoid using unusual words and phrases.
- If you need to use an unusual word or phrase, you can explain the meaning to your users by:
  » Showing the meaning in the text (for example, 'I like bass. A bass is a fish.'); or
  » Showing the meaning in brackets (for example, 'I like bass (a type of fish)'; or
  » Linking the word to a definition on a glossary page on your website; or
  » Linking the word to a definition footnote on the same page.

Tips
If your use of an unusual word always means the same thing, you only have to define it the first time.

If your use of an unusual word changes, you must define the word on every occasion (for example, a bass might be a type of fish in one paragraph and a musical instrument in another).

Always define technical terms and jargon that any user might not understand depending on their familiarity with the subject.

Wherever possible, avoid using jargon and idioms. These are bad for novices in your industry and users who don't natively speak your language.

See Also
- 3.1.4 - Abbreviations
- 3.1.5 - Reading Level
- 3.1.6 - Pronunciation

3.1.4 - Abbreviations
Define any abbreviations.

Using abbreviations can confuse and prevent some of your users from understanding your website. Users with limited memory, cognitive impairments or reliance on screen magnifiers may struggle with shortened words and phrases.

Avoid using abbreviations where you can and explain them when you need to use them.

Abbreviations (like Dr for Doctor) also include acronyms (NATO) and initialisms (FBI).

How to Pass
- Avoid using abbreviations, acronyms and initialisms.
- If you need to use an abbreviation, you can explain the meaning to your users by:
    - » Showing the meaning in the text (for example, Federal Bureau of Investigation (FBI)); or
    - » Linking to a definition on a glossary page on your website; or
    - » Linking to a definition footnote on the same page; or
    - » Using the "abbr" HTML tag.

Tips
The tidiest solution when you need to abbreviate is the HTML option, which creates a hidden expansion that appears on hover and is understood by screen readers.

If your use of an abbreviation always means the same thing, you only have to define it the first time it appears on a page.

If your use changes, you must define the word on every occasion (for example 'Dr' might mean 'Doctor' in one paragraph and 'Drive' as part of an address in another).

Think of creative ways to avoid abbreviations. For example, rather than "FBI" you could use "Federal Bureau of Investigation" once and then "the Bureau" afterwards)

Exceptions

You don't need to explain an abbreviation, acronym or initialism if it's part of the language (for example, "laser" or "CD").

See Also

- 3.1.3 – Unusual Words
- 3.1.5 – Reading Level
- 3.1.6 – Pronunciation

3.1.5 - Reading Level
Ensure users with nine years of schooling can read your content.

All of your users need to be able to read your content. That means you need to write with a range of people in mind, from a College Professor to someone straight out of school.

The key is to write as simply as you can, in clear and plain language, as this will help users with reading and comprehension difficulties.

The generally agreed level to aim for is someone with nine years of schooling, starting from primary education.

How to Pass
Write content that a person with seven to nine years of schooling can understand by:

- Writing the content so someone with no more than nine years of school can understand you (that's nine years from their first day at school, so no college or further education).
- Adding summaries, images and diagrams to content to help explain meaning.
- Breaking up content with well-organised sections and headings.
- Provide a link to supplemental content that further explains complex content.

Tips
You can never write something that every human on the planet will understand.

Short sentences are easiest to understand.

Stick to one topic per paragraph and one thought per sentence.

Avoid slang, jargon and idioms.

Use common words.

Write how people speak.

Use bullet points.

Use active, not passive, language (for example, 'The words were written by Luke' is passive, but 'Luke wrote the words' is active).

Exceptions
You don't need to worry about using correct names, even if they are complicated or hard to read. Names of things like people, films, books and companies all might be hard to read, but they are beyond your control.

See Also
- 3.1.3 - Unusual Words
- 3.1.4 - Abbreviations
- 3.1.6 - Pronunciation

3.1.6 - Pronunciation

Define words where the meaning is ambiguous without pronunciation.

You can help your users by paying attention to words where the meaning isn't clear unless the word is pronounced (or spoken). Words like these can make it hard for your users to understand your content, especially if they use a screen reader which could use incorrect pronunciation or have limited reading comprehension.

This covers words that are spelt the same but pronounced differently (for example, 'bow' v 'bow') - also known as heteronyms.

How to Pass

- Avoid using words where the meaning, in context, is ambiguous without a pronunciation guide.
- If you need to use such a word, you can explain the meaning to your users by:
  » Providing the phonetic pronunciation of words immediately after the word; or
  » Linking the word to a pronunciation guide.

Exceptions

If the correct pronunciation is clear from the context of the sentence (for example "Robin Hood used a bow and arrow").

See Also

- 3.1.3 - Unusual Words
- 3.1.4 - Abbreviations
- 3.1.5 - Reading Level

Guideline 3.2 - Predictable

Make your website appear and act predictably.

This guideline contains seven sections, relating to how your website reacts when users view and operate it.

This includes elements receiving focus and input, navigation, changes, help and controls.

3.2.1 - On Focus

Don't change elements when they receive focus.

All users need predictability when navigating a website. If elements don't act as they expect, they may become disorientated.

In particular, once an element receives focus from a user, whether with a mouse or keyboard, the element must not automatically change (known as 'changing on focus'). This can disorientate users.

A change on focus is especially troublesome for users who navigate by keyboard, as well as those with visual disabilities or cognitive limitations.

How to Pass
- Ensure no element changes purely by receiving focus.
- Avoid both behavioural and visual modifications.
- Ensure that:
  » Links don't open automatically on focus; and
  » Forms don't submit without the user acting (such as clicking the 'Submit' button); and
  » There are no automatic pop-ups; and
  » Focus never jumps to another element automatically; and
  » No other action that occurs on focus alone causes the page to change.

Tips
Most well-made websites will not have any of these errors by default, you would need to choose to add in a change on focus.

A great way to test this guideline is to unplug your mouse and navigate your way around your website with your keyboard. If anything moves, submits or changes on focus, fix it!

Exceptions

Elements can change on focus if the *context* doesn't change. For example, you can use a dynamic menu on your website, the kind where navigation options drop-down when you hover over an item. This is not a change of context.

Another example would be a hover status on a link. Again, this isn't a change of context.

See Also

3.2.2 - On Input

Level A

3.2.2 - On Input
Don't change elements when they receive input.

As we saw with 3.2.1 - On Focus, all users need predictability when navigating a website. If elements don't act as they expect, they may become disorientated.

This is also true when elements receive input, they shouldn't automatically change. For example, forms shouldn't skip to another field or auto-submit without confirmation from the user.

A change on input is especially troublesome for users who navigate by keyboard, as well as those with visual disabilities or cognitive limitations.

How to Pass
Ensure no elements change on input.

Here are some examples of the kinds of things to look out for:

- Forms must not auto-submit when all fields are filled – this prevents your users from checking and editing what they have written.
- Focus must not automatically jump to the next field in a form once a field is complete.
- Using a control must not automatically perform the action (for example, selecting to subscribe to a newsletter in a check box must not automatically subscribe your user, they should be able to click a submit button to confirm their decision).

Exceptions
Elements can change on input if you inform the user of the change before they have the chance to input their data or make their selection. For example, you may have seen websites with options in the header to choose text size. Once you click on the size you want, the website changes without giving you the chance to confirm your choice.

Controls like that don't need to have a submit button if it's clear from the text before the element what will happen when you input.

Tips
The easiest way to pass is to use submit buttons and avoid jumping your users between fields. It's all about leaving control with your users, where it belongs.

See Also
* 3.2.1 - On Focus
* 3.2.5 - Change on Request

Level AA

3.2.3 - Consistent Navigation
Position menus and standard controls consistently.

When you visit a website these days, it's almost second nature to understand where the main menu is and to expect it to be in the same place on every page. Web designers know that having a consistent navigation menu helps users move around websites.

Consistent navigation helps users who may have trouble moving around a website and find themselves 'lost' more often than others. Your users who rely on spatial navigation, due to impaired sight, or need extra help understanding your website benefit most.

This consistency also applies to standard controls of your website – things like your search box or 'Skip to Content' link. Don't move them all over the place, use a consistent template for key elements.

How to Pass
- Keep navigation menus in the same location on all pages; and
- Present the options in navigation menus in the same order on all pages; and
- Keep all other standard controls (for example, your search box) in the same location on all pages.

Tips
Using a standard template for your website will help you meet this guideline.

See Also
- 2.4.1 - Bypass Blocks
- 2.4.5 - Multiple Ways
- 2.4.8 - Location
- 3.2.4 - Consistent Identification

Level AA

3.2.4 - Consistent Identification
Use components with the same function consistently.

It should be obvious that using consistent identification across your website helps your users move around, interact and do what it is you want them to do. Sadly, it's often overlooked and buttons, icons or links with the same function look completely different.

Users with screen readers and screen magnifiers benefit even further from consistent identification. They often use familiarity as a means of understanding and selecting functions. Therefore, elements with the same function should be labelled and appear consistent across your website. This includes visually hidden labels for screen readers.

How to Pass
- Any icons used are consistent (for example, 'Print page' or Instagram link); and
- Elements with the same function are labelled and named consistently; or
- Elements with the same function have a consistent text alternative.

Tips
Consistent is not the same as identical (for example, an arrow icon might link to the next page in a series, but depending on the page the text alternative would be 'Go to page 2' or 'Go to page 3').

An image can have different meanings in different contexts, so require different text alternatives to pass this guideline. For example, a tick icon or check mark can mean both 'fishing line included with purchase' and 'registration form filled in successfully').

See Also
- 1.1.1 - Non-text Content
- 2.4.4 - Link Purpose (In Context)
- 2.4.9 - Link Purpose (Link Only)
- 3.2.2 - Consistent Navigation
- 4.1.2 - Name, Role, Value

Level AAA

3.2.5 - Change on Request
Don't change elements without a request.

Some of your users will find automatic changes hard to deal with. Unexpected actions can interrupt their concentration and prevent them from reaching their goals. Help your users by keeping them in control and avoiding elements on your website that change automatically.

A change without a request is especially troublesome for users who navigate by keyboard, as well as those with visual disabilities or cognitive limitations.

How to Pass
- If you have an element that updates or changes automatically (like a live news ticker), provide an option to pause this and update only when requested.
- All links open in the same window, unless it's essential (for example, opening a transcript to a video).
- If a link does open in a new window, the user is aware of this (for example, in the anchor text of the link or by an icon).
- Forms do not auto-submit when fields are filled.
- Any redirect from one page to another is immediate.

Tips
Avoid using the option to add a pause button wherever possible, it's not as accessible as giving the user full control.

This guideline builds on 2.2.2 - Pause, Stop, Hide and 3.2.2 - On Input by removing some exceptions, so you may already have passed.

The best way to redirect a user from one webpage to another is to do it without them noticing. One of the simplest ways to do this is to edit a website's .htaccess file, which is in the root directory (not all servers will allow you to edit this file, so check with your hosting provider).

See Also
- 2.2.2 - Pause, Stop, Hide
- 3.2.2 - On Input
- 3.3.5 - Help

Level A

3.2.6 - Consistent Help
Present help options in the same order.

Offering help options is great for all users, whether the help is human contact or self-service. Users with disabilities may use help options more than other users and will benefit from the consistent presentation of their choices.

A simple way to achieve this is by adding an email address, phone number or 'contact us' link to your main navigation. You could also offer live chat on every page. The key is to keep these options in the same order wherever they exist.

How to Pass
Where help is offered to users on multiple pages of a website, it is done so in a consistent order.

Tips
Help options can include contact details, a contact form, live chat, FAQs or an automated chatbot.

It's important to note that this doesn't require websites to offer help, just that when help is offered it is done consistently across all pages.

Consistent order means both placement (for example before or after the main page content) and order within a menu (for example phone number before email).

If you're going to pick one thing to do, add a 'Contact' or 'Help' link to your main navigation and present all the help options on that page.

See Also
3.3.5 - Help

Guideline 3.3 - Input Assistance

Help users avoid and correct their mistakes.

This guideline contains eight sections, including identifying errors in input, preventing them as far as possible and offering help to fix them.

This includes input fields, labelling and instructions.

Level A

3.3.1 - Error Identification
Identify and describe input errors for users.

Users of all kinds will make mistakes when using your website, so it's important to clearly identify and describe errors. Input errors include users not providing required information as well as providing information that doesn't meet validation criteria.

Be as specific as possible when highlighting an error, so a user has the best chance of fixing their mistake and continuing. This means doing more than adding a red box around a missed field for example.

How to Pass
- Identify and explain to the user any mistakes that you can detect automatically.
- Add error explanation close to the error, showing what is wrong and how to fix it.

Tips
If a form requires input in a certain format, show and describe the required format.

If a mandatory field is empty, highlight the field and explain what's required.

Build forms to be forgiving, accepting variations on the formats you prefer.

Don't ask for too much information, just what you need.

Be specific. Use clear, concise instruction and form field labels.

Highlight mistakes in forms with colours and symbols.

Don't clear a form if a user makes a mistake. Save the information and allow the user to edit their error and continue.

Provide extra help by giving your contact details on all pages (the header or footer are great) and especially near forms.

See Also
- 1.3.3 - Sensory Characteristics
- 1.4.1 - Use of Colour

- 3.3.2 - Labels or Instructions
- 3.3.3 - Error Suggestion
- 3.3.4 - Error Prevention (Legal, Financial, Data)

Level A

3.3.2 - Labels or Instructions
Provide labels or instructions for user input.

Most websites have at least some elements that require user input. For example, these might be controls or forms. It's essential to label controls such as radio buttons and checkboxes so that users understand what they are selecting.

It can also be useful to provide users with clear instructions around forms and controls, especially if there are validation rules around inputs. Be wary that overdoing instructions can make controls harder to understand.

How to Pass
- Use descriptive labels on form fields and controls.
- Provide text instructions at the beginning of a form or section of a form.
- Show users the expected format of free text entries.
- Indicate required fields.
- Use text to identify required fields that have been missed.

Tips
Keep your labels simple - too much explanation can be counter-productive. Things like 'First name', 'Email' and 'Your message' are fine.

The same goes for instructions, 'Required fields are in red and have a * symbol' works great. So does 'Fill in this form and click 'Submit' to get in touch'.

Think about how your use of colour affects things like required fields if you want to highlight them by colour. Don't highlight by colour alone, pick a symbol too.

Consider error identification and make sure that you give helpful instructions when your users make mistakes on forms.

See Also
- 2.4.6 - Headings and Labels
- 3.3.1 - Error Identification
- 4.1.2 - Name, Role, Value

3.3.3 - Error Suggestion
Suggest corrections when users make mistakes.

All users make mistakes - they're only human after all. When they make mistakes on your website (whether it's their fault or not), they get frustrated.

Input errors are common, especially where fields are mandatory or will only accept input in a specific format. Going beyond identifying errors to suggesting corrections is particularly helpful to users with cognitive or visual limitations.

How to Pass
Ensure that:

- You identify input errors and suggest corrections where possible.
- When the error is missing a required field, communicate this to the user with a text suggestion.
- If the error is in the format of the input, the suggestion shows the correct format (for example, 'The date must be in the form DD/MM/YYYY').
- If the error is because the input needed to be from a limited list of values, provide these values and explain them.

Tips
This guideline builds on 3.3.1 - Error Identification by adding a requirement to make a suggestion for user input to fix errors.

Be specific.

If a user makes an error, provide a list of links that the user can follow to jump back to correct their input.

Make it easy to re-submit incorrect forms by retaining all correct data

Exceptions
You don't need to provide suggestions if:

- It would negatively impact data security; or
- It goes against the purpose of the content.

See Also
- 3.3.1 - Error Identification

- 3.3.4 – Error Prevention (Legal, Financial, Data)
- 3.3.6 – Error Prevention (All)

Level AA

3.3.4 – Prevention (Legal, Financial, Data)
Check, confirm and allow reversal of pages that cause important commitments.

When a user is going through a process that results in a serious financial or legal commitment, or a change in data storage, it's more important than ever to try and prevent mistakes.

Although all users are susceptible to making mistakes, some disabilities and impairments can make users more likely to make errors. For example, people with reading or writing difficulties may type words incorrectly and those with motor disabilities may press keys in error.

Where the errors are legally binding, this can lead to serious consequences.

How to Pass
If a process results in:

- a legal commitment;
- a financial commitment;
- modification or deletion of stored data; or
- submission of test responses

at least one of the following is true:

- submissions are reversible;
- input is checked for errors and users are given a chance to correct mistakes; or
- users are given a chance to review and confirm all input before submitting.

Tips
Remember this covers both submission of data and its deletion.

To make a submission or deletion reversible, provide users with a set time in which they can undo or change the action.

Check for input errors as users enter each field.

Replay all inputs (or the information about to be deleted) to a user and ask them to confirm they are correct before saving the submission.

3.3.6 – Error Prevention (All) widens this guideline to include the submission and deletion of any data, so rather than judging if the submission is financial or legal, apply the solutions to all submissions and deletion requests.

See Also
- 3.3.1 - Error Identification
- 3.3.3 - Error Suggestion
- 3.3.6 - Error Prevention (All)

3.3.5 - Help
Provide help to users.

While many guidelines cover highlighting mistakes and remedying them, it's useful to help users avoid making errors in the first place. Users with disabilities, such as impairments with reading, focus or understanding, are more likely to make mistakes than others.

Where a label or control isn't as clear as it can be, adding contextual help can prevent users from making errors.

How to Pass
Provide contextual help whenever part of a website may be hard to understand.

Tips
For a form, it can be helpful to provide links to contextual help about certain fields. For example, why the question is being asking and the type of response expected.

Where a form field has a required input type or format, explain this.

Help can be by tooltip, a link to a new page or simply a good explanation near the element you're providing help for.

See Also
- 3.3.1 - Error Identification
- 3.3.2 - Labels or Instructions
- 3.3.3 - Error Suggestion
- 3.3.4 - Error Prevention (Legal, Financial, Data)
- 3.3.6 - Error Prevention (All)

3.3.6 - Error Prevention (All)

Check, confirm and allow reversal of pages that require users to submit information.

When a user is going through a process that results in them submitting information, it's more important than ever to try and prevent mistakes.

Although all users are susceptible to making mistakes, some disabilities and impairments can make users more likely to make errors. For example, people with reading or writing difficulties may type words incorrectly and those with motor disabilities may press keys in error.

How to Pass

If a process results in the submission of information, at least one of the following is true:

- submissions are reversible;
- input is checked for errors and users are given a chance to correct mistakes; or
- users are given a chance to review and confirm all input before submitting.

Tips

Remember this covers both submission of data and its deletion.

To make a submission or deletion reversible, provide users with a set time in which they can undo or change the action.

Check for input errors as users enter each field.

Replay all inputs (or the information about to be deleted) to a user and ask them to confirm they are correct before saving the submission.

See Also

- 3.3.1 - Error Identification
- 3.3.3 - Error Suggestion
- 3.3.4 - Error Prevention (Legal, Financial, Data)

3.3.7 - Redundant Entry
Auto-fill or provide information that's required more than once in the same process.

When a user is following a multi-step process, they may need help if information is asked for on more than one step of the process.

Requiring users to remember, re-type or replicate information within a process may be difficult for some users due to the cognitive requirements. Users with memory issues or who experience cognitive fatigue will benefit from fields auto-filling with information entered previously.

How to Pass
If a process requires information that a user has previously provided to be entered again in the same process:

- auto-fill the information; or
- make the information available to select.

Exceptions
- Where re-entering the information is essential
- If the re-entering is required for security
- When information entered previously is no longer valid

Tips
A browser's auto-fill feature is not sufficient.

Your website doesn't need to retain information between distinct sessions for a user.

Making information available could include auto-filling, providing drop down options or a check box to copy across previous responses.

See Also
- 3.3.8 - Accessible Authentication

Level AA

3.3.8 - Accessible Authentication

Don't authenticate users through memory, transcription or cognitive tests without alternatives.

Although it can be important to authenticate users, those with cognitive impairments may have difficulty with remembering passwords or typing in one-time codes.

Some users will be unable to recall a password or series of gestures to access their accounts and require help or alternative means to authenticate.

How to Pass

If you are authenticating a user, avoid:

- asking for a memorised password; or
- requiring them to type in certain characters; or
- making them solve any kind of puzzle, calculation or test.

Exceptions

You can ask a user to complete a cognitive test if you also provide:

- an alternative authentication method that doesn't require a test; or
- help for the user in completing the test; or
- a test which requires the user to identify objects; or
- a test which requires the user to identify non-text content they provided previously.

Tips

Where you use multi-factor authentication, each stage of the process must comply.

Password recovery processes must also meet this guideline.

Personal information such as an email address or phone number is fine to use, as this is consistent across all websites and unique to the user.

Supporting password autofill by browser and password managers is providing help.

Further help could be allowing copy and paste into password fields to reduce re-typing.

Enable users to toggle hidden characters on and off, for example when typing in a password.

Avoid asking for certain characters from a password as this means the user cannot use copy and paste.

You can send an authentication link to a user and skip the need for passwords.

See Also
- 1.3.5 - Identify Input Purpose
- 3.3.9 - Accessible Authentication (Enhanced)
- 4.1.2 - Name, Role, Value

Level AAA

3.3.9 – Accessible Authentication (Enhanced)

Don't authenticate users through memory, transcription or cognitive tests.

Although it can be important to authenticate users, those with cognitive impairments may have difficulty with remembering passwords or typing in one-time codes.

Some users will be unable to recall a password or series of gestures to access their accounts and require help or alternative means to authenticate.

This builds on 3.3.8 – Accessible Authentication by removing the exceptions around identifying objects or non-text content the user had provided.

How to Pass

If you are authenticating a user, avoid:

• asking for a memorised password; or
• requiring them to type in certain characters; or
• making them solve any kind of puzzle, calculation or test.

Exceptions

You can ask a user to complete a cognitive test if you also provide:

• an alternative authentication method that doesn't require a test; or
• help for the user in completing the test.

Tips

Where you use multi-factor authentication, each stage of the process must comply.

Password recovery processes must also meet this guideline.

Personal information such as an email address or phone number is fine to use, as this is consistent across all websites and unique to the user.

Supporting password autofill by browser and password managers is providing help.

Further help could be allowing copy and paste into password fields to reduce re-typing.

Enable users to toggle hidden characters on and off, for example when typing in a password.

Avoid asking for certain characters from a password as this means the user cannot use copy and paste.

You can send an authentication link to a user and skip the need for passwords.

See Also
- 1.3.5 - Identify Input Purpose
- 3.3.8 - Accessible Authentication
- 4.1.2 - Name, Role, Value

Principle 4 – Robust

Produce content in a way that makes it accessible to a wide range of technologies.

Although this principle only has a few requirements, they are wide ranging.

This includes making sure your website is compatible with current and future technologies, setting roles for components, and handling status messages.

Guideline 4.1 - Compatible

Make your website as compatible as possible with a wide range of technologies.

This guideline contains just two sections, relating to assigning name, role and value to elements, and managing the display of status messages.

4.1.2 - Name, Role, Value
Ensure the name and role of user components can be understood by technology.

Users who rely on assistive technology, such as a screen reader or magnifier, rely on their technology being able to correctly understand and interact with the components of your website.

For the most part, using standard controls such as those in HTML enables most technologies to interpret and control your website.

However, if you have built custom controls, it's essential they can still be processed by assistive technology.

How to Pass
- Ensure every component of your website has a name, role or label (this can be visible or hidden).
- Where a component has a value (for example a radio button can be selected or unselected), the value can be determined by technology.

Tips
A common value is whether an element has focus or not at a given time, and whether that state has changed.

Elements to pay keen attention to include forms and links.

Remember, standard HTML will almost always pass 4.1.2 - Name, Role, Value without further work.

Be wary of third-party plugins or code and make sure these meet the criteria.

Run your website through a HTML validator to spot any minor coding issues to fix.

Level AA

4.1.3 - Status Messages
Alert users to changes in content that aren't given focus.

Users with visual impairments and low vision can benefit from status messages to inform them of changes, results or processes that aren't clear from a change of context. Adding clear messages can help these users understand and gain further context about the action they're taking.

Assigning a role to a status message means that it can be announced by screen reader or other assistive technology.

How to Pass

A 'status message' is a special term used for these guidelines, meaning something that provides information to the user on the:

- results of an action;
- waiting state of an application;
- progress of a process; or
- existence of errors.

The message is also defined as one not delivered by a change in context.

Where you use a status message, ensure it as assigned an appropriate ARIA role of "status" or "alert".

Tips

This can be a little difficult to understand, so here's an example:

A user searches the website for store locations.

The list of results is a change in context, so not a 'status message'.

However, a text displayed about the status of the search such as "Now searching..." would be a 'status message'.

Conformance Claims

Congratulations on creating a website that meets one of the three levels of conformance set out by the Web Content Accessibility Guidelines.

If you've done that, whether it's Level A, AA or AAA, you've made excellent progress.

The hard work is done and there's no requirement for you to make a conformance claim, display any badge or get a certificate from anyone.

However, you may wish to make a conformance claim to the W3C and record your level of conformance for a range of reasons, including legal or public relations.

The basis for a claim

Conformance claims are made at individual webpage level but I recommend ensuring your full website complies before claiming.

To make a conformance claim, you must:

- Have fulfilled all the guidelines for the level you are claiming (including all of any lower level)
- Ensure all parts of all pages conform, including all sections of any process such as a checkout, or provide a conforming alternative version
- Ensure your conformance is based on accessible technologies (everything in this book counts as an accessible technology)

Making a claim

If you choose to make a conformance claim public, you must state:

- The date of your claim
- The title, version and URL of the guidelines you have followed (available on the W3C website)
- Your conformance level (A, AA or AAA)

- A description of the pages for which the claim is made (usually, your entire website)
- A list of the technologies relied upon (for example HTML, CSS, etc)

Getting Started

Now that you've read this guide (or skipped ahead to see if there's a cheat code - sorry, there isn't), what's next?

I hope I've given you the knowledge to get started on updating or creating your website in line with the Web Content Accessibility Guidelines - now and in the future.

Understanding the principles and guidelines will give you the foundational skills to design and plan with web accessibility in mind - a much better place to be than trying to hack together solutions later on.

Even if you're feeling unsure, I encourage you to get started - better is better, you don't need to be perfect at the first attempt.

A good place to start is an automated checker. While these are no replacement for expertise and human reviews, they can be good for giving you a priority order of issues to fix.

Here are a few free options I recommend:

WAVE - a free service from WebAIM and launched all the way back in 2001.
http://wave.webaim.org

W3C Markup Validation Service - a free service directly from W3C that helps validate the markup of web documents.
https://validator.w3.org

There are of course many paid services too, but rather than list any in a book I'm always happy to have a pre-look at any you might be considering - just send an email to luke@wuhcag.com.

With the paid services, I will always advise caution. Use them for what they are - a way to get started and focus your efforts, but never rely on them without a developer's oversight if you're serious about truly reaching a level of compliance.

However you get started, thank you for reading this guide and I wish you the best of luck in your projects.

If you're interested in having this book in a digital format, taking a course or joining a Discord of fellow readers, you can find out more at www.wuhcag.com.

As a thank you for buying this book, forward the receipt from wherever you bought it to luke@wuhcag.com and you'll get the same amount discounted off any package at Wuhcag - I'll even double the discount if you've left a review on Amazon.

One last thing. If you have found this book useful, please consider sharing it with others to help spread the word and make the web a more accessible place for all.

www.ingramcontent.com/pod-product-compliance
Lightning Source LLC
Chambersburg PA
CBHW011845200326
41597CB00028B/4716